Fortress · 19

Crusader Castles of the Teutonic Knights (2)

The stone castles of Latvia and Estonia 1185–1560

Stephen Turnbull · Illustrated by Peter Dennis

Series editors Marcus Cowper and Nikolai Bogdanovic

First published in Great Britain in 2004 by Osprey Publishing, Elms Court, Chapel Way, Botley, Oxford OX2 9LP, United Kingdom.
Email: info@ospreypublishing.com

ISBN 1 84176 712 3

SERIES EDITORS: Marcus Cowper and Nikolai Bogdanovic

Editorial: Ilios Publishing, Oxford, UK (www.iliospublishing.com)
Maps by The Map Studio
Design: Ken Vail Graphic Design, Cambridge, UK
Index by Alison Worthington
Originated by The Electronic Page Company, Cwmbran, UK
Printed and bound by L-Rex Printing Company Ltd.

04 05 06 07 08   10 9 8 7 6 5 4 3 2 1

A CIP catalogue record for this book is available from the British Library.

FOR A CATALOGUE OF ALL BOOKS PUBLISHED BY OSPREY MILITARY AND AVIATION PLEASE CONTACT:

Osprey Direct UK, PO Box 140, Wellingborough,
Northants, NN8 2FA, United Kingdom.
Email: info@ospreydirect.co.uk

Osprey Direct USA, c/o MBI Publishing, PO Box 1,
729 Prospect Ave, Osceola, WI 54020, USA.
Email: info@ospreydirectusa.com

www.ospreypublishing.com

Glossary

Anwalt	Advocate
Chapter-general	a council attended by all the brethren
Cogge	a type of ship used by the Order
Dansk	detached latrine or sewage tower
Grosskomtur	grand commander
Grosschaffer	(Minister of Trade) in charge of developing commerce
Hauskomtur	house commander
Hochmeister	High Master
Iarbusse	a form of severe punishment
Deutschmeister	German master
Komtur	commander of a castle
Komtureis	commanderies, the administrative area of the Order's lands
Landkomtur	district commander
Landmeister	provincial master
Marschall	Marshal, responsible for leading the Order into battle
Reyza	a raid by crusaders into pagan territory
Sword Brother	a member of Order of the Militia of Christ
Traction trebuchet	A catapult operated by manpower
Tressler	Treasurer

Artist's note

Editor's note

Unless otherwise indicated, all the images in this book are the property of the author.

Dedication

To Suzy Farry.

Author's note

I would like to thank all those who have helped me in the preparation of this book, including the curators of the castles and museums depicted here in Lithuania, Latvia and Estonia. I would particularly like to thank Neil Taylor of Regent Travel Ltd, the specialists in Baltic travel, for his advice and materials. William Urban, the author of so many fine books about the medieval Baltic, supplied me with much unique source material. Emma Farry helped greatly with translation. Above all I wish to thank my late wife Jo, whose support never failed in spite of the illness that prevented her from going to Latvia with me to see for herself the crusader castles of the Teutonic Knights.

Preface

The Teutonic Knights of Germany are best known for their crusading activities in Prussia and their cataclysmic defeat at the battle of Tannenberg in 1410. But throughout its existence the Teutonic Order had also a northern branch that was active in the land known to contemporary chroniclers as Livonia. The boundaries of the Teutonic Order's Livonian state changed several times as it expanded and contracted, so it is difficult to be precise about its borders. In general, however, 'Livonia' corresponds to the whole of modern Latvia and all but the northern part of Estonia. It also sometimes incorporated portions of Lithuania and western Russia. The term 'Livonia' will be used throughout this work with more precise locations being given where appropriate. Livonia was regarded as a cold and distant posting compared with Prussia. Its social and cultural life was simpler, with fewer banquets and parades, but just as in Prussia the Order maintained a complex network of fine crusader castles located primarily along the major rivers. Many of them still exist today. This book tells the story of these castles from their creation until the time when they passed out of the ownership of the Teutonic Order during the 1560s. Unlike the red-brick Prussian castles covered in Volume 1 of this work, the main building material in Livonia was stone, and there was also a difference in the way the crusader castle network was created. In Prussia there was a clear developmental pattern laid down by the Order itself, but in Livonia only a few castles were actually built by the Teutonic Knights. Most were inherited from the extinct Order of Swordbrothers, captured from enemies, acquired by treaty or even purchased from their original owners.

Contents

The castle builders of Livonia

The first crusaders and their castles

By the mid-16th century all the fortresses described in this volume belonged unquestionably to the Teutonic Knights. However, that is not actually how they started out as the first crusader castles of Livonia predated by a few years the foundation of the Teutonic Order in the Holy Land in 1190. The Livonian castles owe their origins instead to a different order of crusader knights that was called into being because of problems associated with the establishment of Christian missionary activity in Latvia during the 1180s. Latvia was a place far from the sun-baked wilderness of the Middle East. It was a hostile, cold and swampy environment that taxed missionary zeal to its utmost limits.

Much of our knowledge of these early days comes from two important contemporary chronicles. The first is the *Chronicle of Henry of Livonia*, who was an eyewitness to many of the extraordinary events he describes in his book of 1229. The historical record continues in the later *Livonian Rhymed Chronicle*, completed between 1290 and 1297. The creation and employment of castles is treated as an important topic in both narratives.

Henry of Livonia begins his chronicle by telling us about a certain Meinhard, a canon of the Augustinian monastery of Segeburg in Holstein. Meinhard had heard stories from sailors and merchants who had travelled up the great Daugava (Dvina) River on which Riga now stands to trade with the pagan tribesmen known as the Livs and the Letts. The worthy canon decided to venture there himself to convert the people to Christianity, even though he was already 'an elderly man with venerable grey hair'. Some converts were made, and in about 1184 Meinhard built a church in the village of Uexkull (Ikskile) and baptised a few Livs. But his new flock were highly vulnerable to attacks from hostile tribesmen. The most serious threat came from across the border in Lithuania, whose inhabitants were to remain stubbornly pagan until the late 14th century, except for brief periods when their rulers accepted Christianity for reasons of political expediency. Meinhard experienced their

The ruins of the castle of Uexkull (Ikskile) viewed from the bank of the Daugava River. Uexkull was the first castle and the first stone building in Latvia. The rise in the water level has safeguarded the ruins at the price of inaccessibility.

hostility for himself when a Lithuanian raid was mounted that winter. The assault forced him to flee to the forests along with the local people. Henry of Livonia takes the story on:

> When the Lithuanians had withdrawn, Meinhard accused the Livonians of foolishness, because they had no fortifications. He promised them that castles would be built if they decided to become and to be considered as sons of God. This pleased them and they promised and confirmed by an oath that they would receive baptism.

Meinhard kept his side of the bargain, and stonemasons were brought over from Gotland the next summer. The result was Latvia's first castle, and in fact its first stone building of any sort. But when the castle of Uexkull was finished the gratitude faded. Many of those who had been baptised relapsed while others refused to accept the faith. Undaunted, Meinhard battled on with his mission, and at least had the satisfaction of seeing his gift of a castle prove its worth when it was attacked by pagan tribesmen from nearby Semgallia (modern Zemgale in southern Latvia).

Meinhard was consecrated Bishop of Uexkull in 1186. His mission spread, but he was to suffer a further disappointment from the inhabitants of nearby Holm (Salaspils). They had also accepted the gift of a castle but had then attacked Meinhard and tried to drive him out of Livonia. The supposed converts then symbolically scrubbed off the waters of baptism in the Daugava River. Local resentment grew, and soon Meinhard and his fellow priests were virtually prisoners of their former flock.

Meinhard died in 1196 and was replaced in the Livonian diocese by Berthold, the Cistercian Abbot of Loccum. It was clearly not a popular posting because Berthold only accepted under protest. His misgivings were well founded, because when he tried to convert the Livonians a plot was hatched to murder him. Berthold was not the sort to take such intimidation lying down, and changed his approach to missionary work in a very dramatic fashion. Henceforth his missionary effort would be backed up by force, so he sailed secretly to Saxony and then returned to Livonia with a crusading army. On 24 July 1198 the first battle took place between native Livonians and the German crusaders who had come to enforce the conversions:

Plan of Holm (Salaspils) on the Daugava. Holm provides an early example of a simple walled area. It was the second castle to be associated with Bishop Meinhard and dates from about 1186. Excavations have revealed a design of an almost perfect square of stone walls with a tower at one corner. It was protected on three sides by a ditch, and on the fourth by the waters of the Daugava.

> The Livonians shouted and yelled in pagan fashion. The Saxon battle lines were armed to fight against them and rushed headlong in an attack upon them. The bishop, restraining his horse badly, was carried by its speed into the midst of the fugitives. Two of the Livonians seized him. A third, Ymaut by name, pierced him from the back with a lance, and the others tore him to pieces, limb from limb.

Astonishingly, Bishop Berthold was one of the few Christian casualties in a victory won partly because the crusaders had heavy cavalry that brushed aside the lighter Livonian ponies. Also, fortunately for the crusaders, one of the triumphant Livonians who had assaulted Berthold's party had placed a captured German

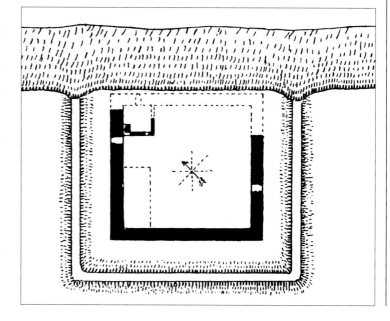

helmet on his own head. This led his comrades to think that the crusaders had advanced against them so they withdrew.

The crusader army then laid waste the Livonian crops in revenge for the loss of the bishop. Much alarmed, the Livonians proposed a truce and called the clergy to them. About 50 pagans were baptised there and then, and about 100 more at Uexkull the following day. Believing that their crusade had been a success the German army sailed for home, but no sooner had they gone than the Livonians performed the ritual of scrubbing off their baptism. Once more the mission had been flung into reverse, and matters deteriorated so much by the year 1199 that Christian priests in Livonia were being hunted down like animals. The missionary enterprise in Latvia seemed to be over.

Medieval Livonia, showing how the lands were divided up between the Teutonic Order and the church. The castles discussed in this work are shown, as are the principle battle sites. (© Osprey Publishing Ltd).

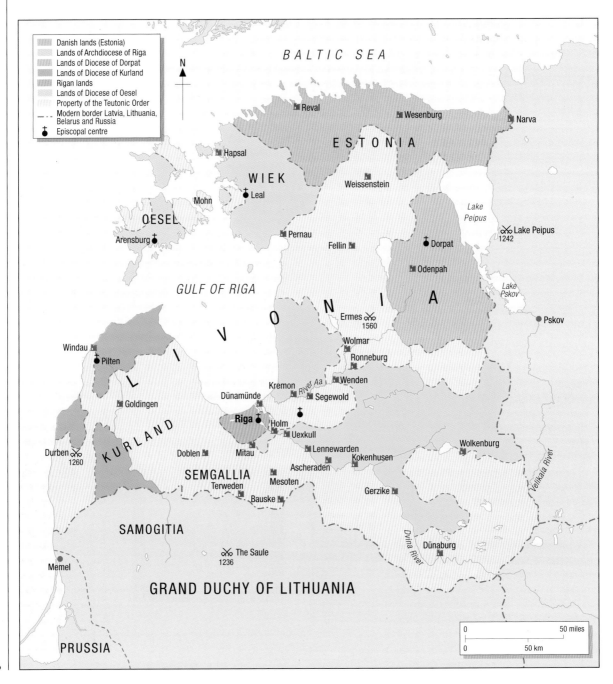

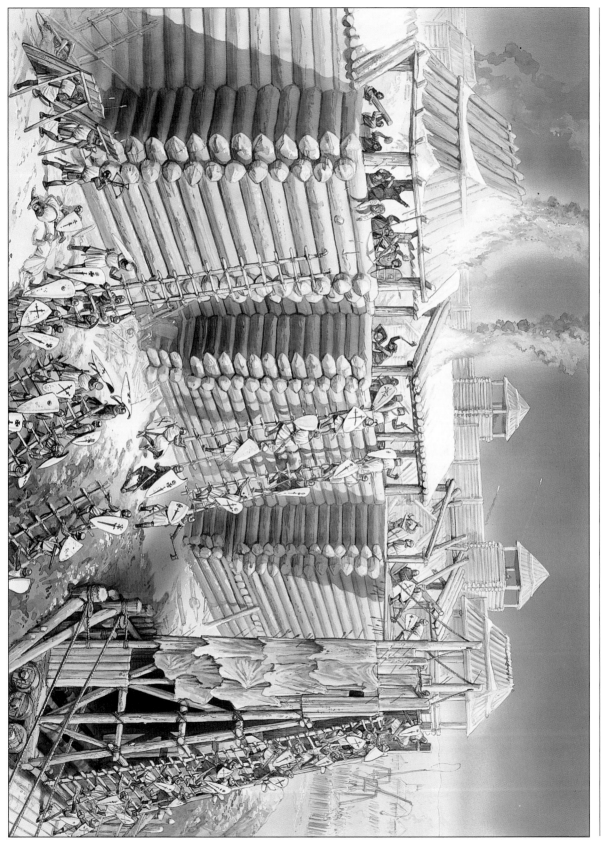

This plate shows the attack by crusaders on a typical pagan timber fortress of Livonia. The incident is the siege of Fellin (Viljandi) in 1211. Fellin was the stronghold of the Saccalians and the key to southern Estonia. The initial attack on Fellin went against the Swordbrothers even though the crusaders had the advantage of their crossbow archery. Siege towers, fire and stone-throwing catapults were then brought into action.

Fellin is shown as a very solid stockade with high walls built on a hill. Vertical support is supplied by massive tree trunks buried securely in the ground, around which a framework of interlocking timbers is raised. Careful cutting near the ends produces a neat and solid joint rather like the traditional log cabin of the American West. The towers are roofed over with shingles above projecting beams. Wooden castles like this were adopted by the crusaders until they could replace them with stone, but similar structures continued to be built and used as temporary forts for many years.

The Swordbrothers are shown in their characteristic livery of a red cross and sword on white. Among the weapons they are using is a man-powered traction trebuchet.

Bishop Albert the castle builder

The late Bishop Berthold of Uexkull was replaced in his frontier diocese by one of the most remarkable characters in Baltic history. His name was Albert of Buxhovden, and a statue of him now stands inside the courtyard of Riga cathedral. Albert arrived in Livonia with very different intentions from those of his two predecessors. He came not as a preacher but as a prince, and was to prove to be one of the great empire-builders and church magnates of the 13th century.

Having absorbed the lesson of Berthold's fate, Albert arrived in his diocese accompanied by a sizeable army of Saxon crusaders and with his legal position secured through privileges granted to him by the Holy Roman Emperor and the Pope. One important concession involved his use of crusaders. Albert was to be allowed to send for reinforcements without asking special permission from the Pope. When he began to exercise these rights he created what became known as the 'perpetual crusade' of annual summer expeditions from Lübeck to Livonia. His crusaders served for two years in return for the promise of a crusader's indulgence (the forgiveness of sins), and year after year Albert journeyed back to Saxony to raise another levy of militant pilgrims. There was no shortage of supply, because Germany had recently experienced a bitter episode of civil war following the death of Emperor Henry in 1197. The conflict had produced a large crop of men with murder or bloodshed on their consciences who were more than eager to have their sins forgiven by service in a crusade.

Albert also realised that his diocese of Uexkull, defended by the castle of the same name, was located too far up the Daugava (Dvina) River to be really effective. So he placed Uexkull into the care of a colleague and founded another castle nearer the sea at the point where a small stream joined the Daugava to form a natural harbour. That was the beginning of the city of Riga. He also founded an outlying castle called Dünamünde at the mouth of the Daugava for the convenience of crusaders arriving from Germany.

Bishop Albert went back to Germany every year until 1224 to drum up support and keep the crusading spirit alive. But at a much earlier stage, indeed by the year 1202, he had realised that the presence of a standing army based in Livonia rather than short-term crusaders would be a great help. The

The two towers of Bauske (Bauska) viewed from inside the courtyard of the palace of the Duke of Kurland. This would have been the view from outside during the medieval period.

problem was that for a secular knight the rewards of campaigning in the Baltic area were not great enough to ensure a long-term commitment. A short period of duty and an indulgence was enough for most men. The permanent life was far better suited to members of the knightly orders such as the Templars. They were sworn to hardship and hard work, and there was plenty of both waiting in Livonia. But when they were approached the established crusading orders were reluctant to spread their limited resources too thinly, so Albert did the only thing possible. He founded an order of his own: the Brothers of the Militia of Christ – otherwise known as the Swordbrothers. They wore a white mantle with the red insignia of a cross and a sword.

A display in the Latvia History Museum showing the method of timber construction used in the building of fortifications prior to the introduction of stone castles by the crusaders.

The Swordbrothers' primary duty was to provide security for the priests and missionaries to do their work, but the nature of the Livonian frontier immediately presented them with a subtle moral challenge to their assumed role. Unlike Muslims in the Holy Land, the Livs and Letts were not in possession of lands or shrines that had once been Christian. So was there any moral justification for attacking them? There was also the practical issue of the division of conquered territory. It was agreed that if further crusades acquired more territory, the Swordbrothers were to garrison what was won using the castles that now began to appear. Over the next few years the number of castles grew to form the line that is nowadays marked by a chain of ruins along the Daugava. But garrison duty did not necessarily imply ownership, and as early as 1204 Albert insisted that only one-third of any new territory could be retained by the Order. The rest had to be handed over to the bishop.

The first battle in which the Swordbrothers took part occurred in 1205 as a response to a hostile move from Lithuania. Viesthard, the leader of the friendly local Semgallian tribes whose lands were being devastated by the Lithuanians, came to Riga and chided the Swordbrothers for having allowed their borders to be overrun. The brethren were reluctant to go to war because Bishop Albert was currently absent, but Viesthard persuaded them in this direction, and a trap was set for the Lithuanians as they returned laden with booty. The ambush was a success and the Lithuanian leader was beheaded. 'God sent such fear into the Lithuanians that they were so dazzled by the German arms that they turned away on all sides', wrote Henry of Livonia.

Military operations recommenced in the spring of 1206 when Bishop Albert was confronted by Russian hostility in the shape of Duke Vladimir of Polozk, who demanded tribute from the inhabitants of the Daugava from his fortress far upstream. Vladimir chose his moment well to enforce his claim, having waited until the crusaders whose terms of service had just expired had sailed for home. The remaining crusaders and the permanent garrison of Swordbrothers were surprised by the sudden arrival of Russians down the Daugava, but managed to beat them off.

The Swordbrothers faced a further attack from Lithuania the following year. This one was launched during the winter, and the outcome served to illustrate the value of the newly established castle line. The Swordbrothers and their local allies assembled at the castle of Lennewarden (Lielvarde) on the northern banks of the Daugava. The Lithuanian army crossed on the ice and challenged their enemies to battle. The crusaders responded and defeated the Lithuanians, after which they pursued them for a whole day, liberating many captives on the way.

LEFT **The first stone castle in Latvia – Uexkull (Ikskile) on the Daugava River 1185**
The first stone building of any sort in Latvia is reconstructed here. This is the castle of Uexkull. We know from the chronicle of Henry of Livonia that the basic structure of the castle was stones held together by mortar. Compared with later castles, Uexkull was just a simple walled enclosure with integral buildings. Only the outer walls make it look like a conventional castle, but the site of this strange new building must have greatly impressed the natives. As befits men who were monks as well as knights, the chapel occupies a sizeable portion of the area. Note the simple garderobe in place of the more elaborate sewage towers seen later in Prussia. To the rear the garrison have created a vegetable garden on the edge of the forest.

It was a model campaign, and indicated the strategy that was to be adopted to counter any further raids from across the Daugava. Albert knew that he had little chance of intercepting a raiding party as it entered Livonia, but at least he could send out timely warnings to the communities who were most likely to be affected. The key to successful communications lay with the chain of castles along the river. Local militia could gather at the castle nearest to the raiders' likely return route and then pursue and attack the heavily laden Lithuanians.

The castle line expands

Apart from the odd pitched battle (which the natives always tried to avoid because of the Order's superiority in heavy cavalry) and several sieges, the wars of the Livonian crusade consisted of savage raids characterised by merciless fighting and atrocities on both sides. Nevertheless, when raids were curtailed most of the native people began to appreciate that there were some advantages in having the Swordbrothers as efficient protectors. But not all the natives responded so favourably to the Swordbrothers' success. For example, Vetseke, who owned the original timber fortress of Kokenhusen (Koknese) was most reluctant to hand the site over to the Swordbrothers. Vetseke believed that the arrival of the crusaders was an unnecessary challenge to his authority in the region, and when German workmen arrived to demolish the castle and rebuild it in stone he massacred them:

Almost all the Germans had gone out to their work and were quarrying rocks in the moat for the building of the fort. They had, in the meantime, laid their swords and arms outside

TOP RIGHT The defence of a Latgallian fortress, from a painting in the Latvia History Museum, Riga. On the hill in the background may be seen the typical outline of a timber hillfort. Such places were the crusaders' first targets.

BOTTOM RIGHT An artist's impression of the probable appearance of the original foundation of Riga in about the year 1210. The city is enclosed by a stone wall. In the left foreground is St George's castle. Bishop Albert's cathedral appears centre left.

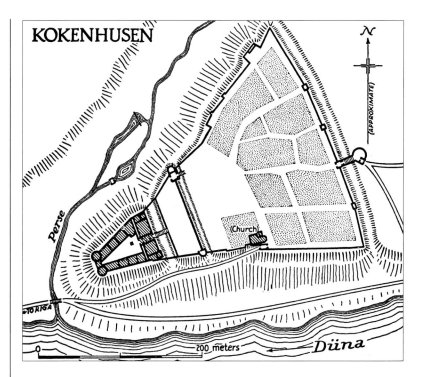

Plan of Kokenhusen (Koknese), showing how the outer bailey grew to enclose the town inside its walls and towers.

the moat, for looking upon the king as their lord and father, they did not fear him. Suddenly all the men and servants of the king ran up, picked up the swords and arms of the Germans and killed many of them as they stood unarmed and naked at their work.

Needless to say, King Vetseke was not allowed to escape unpunished, and the vital rebuilding was completed without his support. The new policy of depending on a fortified line went some way to creating a time of peace along the Daugava frontier that allowed the Order to pursue internal matters concerning its relationship with Bishop Albert. The greatest source of friction between the two parties was the agreement made when the Order was founded concerning the division of newly conquered territories. Fresh concern now arose because of the Swordbrothers' desire to advance the Christian frontier in a completely different direction from the Daugava. That river had long been Albert's chief concern, but another river flowed down towards Riga from the north. This was the Livonian Aa, now called the Gauja. Any move in that direction would ultimately take the Swordbrothers into Estonia. Bishop Albert had little interest in invading Estonia because that area had already been promised to King Waldemar II of Denmark. In addition some parts of Estonia paid tribute to the Russian prince of Pskov, whose daughter had married Albert's brother.

The Swordbrothers cared nothing for such political niceties. The current head of the Order, one Master Wenno, saw an ideal opportunity to convert the comparatively weak tribes of the Aa and greatly resented any interference from the bishop in the process. So the advance north was made without his

Plan of Segewold (Sigulda). Segewold untilises every inch of space available to it on its rocky plateau. Its overall shape is therefore highly irregular, being determined only by the topography of its ground plan. The main entrance to Segewold, on its southern side, has been superbly and sensitively restored to give a stunning impression of this aspect of a Livonian castle. Inside the courtyard the buildings of the convent make use of the outer wall because of lack of space.`

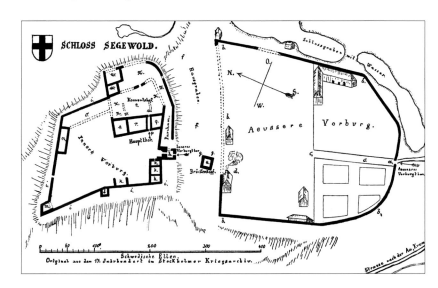

permission. First the native fortress of Treiden (Turaida) was taken and occupied. Then the castle of Segewold (Sigulda) was founded in 1208 on the other side of the deep wooded Aa valley. In the same year the castle of Wenden (Cesis) was founded further upstream. This grew to be a mighty fortress, and Master Wenno made it the headquarters of the Swordbrothers. A certain Wickbert was placed in charge, but he was sympathetic towards Bishop Albert's position so Wenno soon replaced him with another.

This caused the greatest scandal in the history of the Swordbrothers. The ousted Wickbert fled to the protection of Albert in Riga, and in 1209 showed his feelings in no uncertain fashion when he took an axe and smashed in the head of Master Wenno. Wickbert was immediately arrested and tortured on the rack. As the *Livonian Rhymed Chronicle* has it, 'they put him to death as people should traitors'. Needless to say, the murder of the Master of the Swordbrothers by one of his followers caused a huge outrage, and questions began to be asked about the quality of the men who belonged to the Order.

The advance into Estonia

By the year 1211 the threats from Lithuanians to the east, Kurs from pagan Kurland (Kurzeme) in the west who raided Riga by sea, the unconverted Estonians to the north and the odd rebellious Livonian, prompted Albert and the Order to bury their differences. Southern Estonia had to be secured to safeguard their northern flank, regardless of the feelings of the King of Denmark. Alliances were made with potential Russian rivals and then the crusader army, with the Swordbrothers as its core, loyal Livs and Letts in its company and Albert's brother-in-law Engelbert von Thisenhusen at its head, invaded southern Estonia.

Their objective was Fellin (Viljandi), the stronghold of the Saccalians. A fierce siege (described below) was concluded with a negotiated settlement, arranged through the usual conditions of the pagans accepting baptism. The siege of Fellin was a great success for the Order and the stronghold was destined to become one of its greatest castles, but the Swordbrothers initially lacked the resources to garrison a castle so deep in enemy territory. However, the following year the Estonians most obligingly mounted a raid down the Aa against Treiden (Turaida). The Swordbrothers realised their opportunity to destroy the flower of Saccalian warriorhood and marched to Treiden's relief with drums beating. They were met by a shower of spears flying through the air which the crusaders caught on their shields. They then went in with the sword. Perhaps as many as 2,000 Saccalians fell in the battle. Fellin could now be safely included within the Swordbrothers' territory.

It was also during the cold winter of 1211/12 that the Swordbrothers made the surprising and important discovery that winter was the best season for warfare. The swamps froze, the undergrowth was less solid and the natives had difficulty covering their tracks. The mounted German knights could also use the frozen rivers as highways. This was to transform their operations. These techniques came to the fore in a series of campaigns that lasted until 1218 when the Order subjugated the rest of southern Estonian while beating off counter-attacks from

The original Treiden (Turaida) castle as built by the Swordbrothers. Treiden was unique in Latvia in that stone provided little more than the foundations. The remainder of the superstructure was made from red bricks, thus producing an edifice that resembled the Teutonic Order's castles in Prussia. The most distinctive feature of Treiden was its huge chimney-like red-brick tower with a conical roof. This has been reconstructed and is the most striking feature of the site today. The walls and the top of the tower were battlemented.

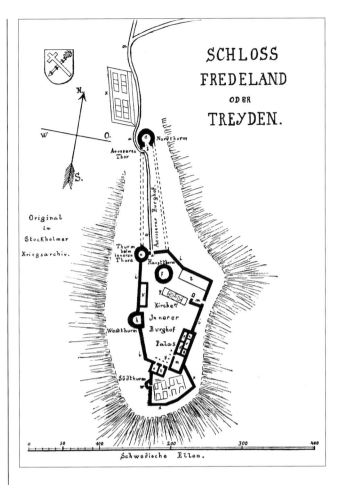

Plan of Treiden (Turaida) in the 16th century. It is generally agreed that the original 13th-century castle consisted of an long, narrow and irregularly walled enclosure with a chapel built into the wall. The castle grew to resemble the conventional convent buildings with the addition of a multi-storey artillery tower of semicircular cross section.

Russians and Lithuanians. The Swordbrothers were now ready for the final conquest of the rest of Estonia, but in 1219 King Waldemar of Denmark pre-empted them by invading Estonia himself from the north. With the full co-operation of Bishop Albert the Danes defeated the pagans at the site that later became known as Reval (Tallinn), the future capital of Estonia.

In 1222, through an agreement acceptable to everyone except the Swordbrothers, Estonia was partitioned between King Waldemar and Bishop Albert. Livonia was beginning to take shape, but the brothers were not satisfied with their possession of only some of the pieces of the complex territorial jigsaw. The bone of contention had always been the rule that when the Swordbrothers conquered new territories they could only keep one-third of it for themselves and hand over the remainder to the bishop. This lack of territory caused financial problems for the Order and their attempts to squeeze more out of the peasants led to a revolt in 1222. The brutal way in which it was put down drew a rebuke from the Pope. The Swordbrothers then tried to seize the Danish lands in northern Estonia, but when only a little had been gained the visiting papal legate made them give it back. However, as soon as he had returned the brothers occupied the lands again and even started encroaching on to Bishop Albert's share. They also began levying tolls on traffic on the Daugava.

The death of Bishop Albert in 1229 lifted the one restraining hand on the Swordbrothers' activities. On a more legitimate level Kurland (Kurzeme) was conquered and converted by them in 1230, but the view was being formed at a high ecclesiastical level that the Swordbrothers had outlived their usefulness. A newly appointed papal legate, Bernard of Aulne, decided that they should be suppressed. But when he tried to recapture the Danish castle at Reval from them he was defeated and taken prisoner. This was hardly the way to treat the Pope's representative.

Master Volkwin of the Swordbrothers began to worry about the Order's future, and came upon a possible solution. In Prussia another order of knighthood had begun a campaign against natives that was being conducted in a similar manner to the wars that the Swordbrothers had waged in Livonia. They were the Teutonic Knights, who had been invited into Prussia by a Polish nobleman. Volkwin proposed that the Swordbrothers should be absorbed into the new, powerful and promising Teutonic Order. When the request was received a delegation from the Teutonic Knights went to Livonia on a tour of inspection, and reported back that the Swordbrothers were not worth bothering with.

There was more than a little touch of hypocrisy about the Teutonic Knights' denunciation of the Swordbrothers. The Teutonic Order had only become active in Baltic affairs after being kicked out of Hungary for similar acts of territorial aggression! Nor were their methods of raiding pagan villages, slaughtering the men and carrying off women and children as captives much different either. But the Teutonic Knights had their future to consider. Prussia was a fresh start, and to be saddled with the responsibility of the Swordbrothers' failures was not in their long-term interests.

In 1234 a damning report on the Swordbrothers was presented to Pope Gregory IX. It began with an account of the attack on Reval, when 100 of the legate's men had perished while trying to enforce the papal will on the Swordbrothers, and:

> They had heaped the bodies into a pile, and had stuck one of the slain who had been too faithful to the Church on top of the other dead to represent the Lord Pope, and had subverted the Church by roundly refusing to allow the Master to hand them over for burial, so that, in due course, converts and others might come and behold this manner of spectacle, and the Brothers might thus be seen by converts, Russians, pagans and heretics to be greater than the Roman Church.

The catalogue of other abuses included enlisting Russians and pagans to fight for them, killing 401 converts, beating up the Cistercian monks of Dünamünde, pillaging the bishop's lands, preventing aspiring Christians from receiving baptism from the bishop and taking others as slaves. The damage to property alone was calculated precisely as 40,500 marks.

The Pope ordered the Swordbrothers to appear before him during the winter of 1235/36 to answer the charges. The judgement handed down from the session was that the Swordbrothers should return their captured lands in Estonia to their previous owners. They also had to pay compensation for all the losses they had caused through battles, ransoms and lost incomes. The proposed punishment was so severe that it made the Swordbrothers' abolition almost inevitable. Yet within a few months neither punishment nor abolition was necessary, because the Swordbrothers had carried out both for themselves.

The Teutonic Knights take over

The immediate stimulus for the destruction of the Swordbrothers was the arrival in 1236 in Riga of an army of 2,000 German crusaders eager for battle against Lithuania, where a new and formidable ruler called Mindaugas had arisen. Master Volkwin of the Swordbrothers knew that he did not have the resources for the task, but he could not send the crusaders home without some

View of Bauske castle from the modern bridge showing the clear outlines of the earthwork angle bastion. Bauske (Bauska) is built on a promontory where the two rivers Memele and Musa meet.

15

A painting in the Latvia Military Museum in Riga showing the battle of the Saule in 1236, the fateful conflict that destroyed the Swordbrothers and allowed the Teutonic order to begin its long hegemony in Livonia.

action. So Volkwin compromised by agreeing to lead a raid into Samogitia (modern Zemaitija or Lower Lithuania). As the area chosen was far from Mindaugas' headquarters Volkwin hoped that he could achieve surprise both for an attack and for a rapid withdrawal. The operation was no minor raid as Volkwin had assembled 100 knights and 1,200 footsoldiers. There were also 1,500 natives and 200 Russians from Pskov in addition to the visiting crusaders. Most of the senior members of the Swordbrothers were also present. At first all went well, as related in *The Livonian Rhymed Chronicle*, our only source for the fateful campaign near the Saule River in 1236:

> They put together a large and handsome army and rode to Lithuania through the fields and over many streams, suffering great hardships until they finally came to that land. There many a glorious band robbed and burned and ravaged freely up and down the countryside. They then turned back towards the Saule, moving through the marshes and moors

But Mindaugas knew what was going on. The delay in the crusaders' movements had been just sufficient for him to move his army into a position where he could cut off the crusader army on its return. The Lithuanians caused utter confusion in the crusader camp, and Master Volkwin was particularly furious at the behaviour of the visitors from Germany:

> The master rode up to the best of them and said, 'Now is the time to fight! Our honour is at stake! If we immediately attack them now, then we can safely ride back home again.' But the worthy heroes said, 'We do not wish to fight here. If we should lose our horses we would have to use our feet.' The master replied, 'Well then, would you like to lose your heads as well as your horses?'

A reconstruction of Terweden (Tervete) castle, the most important pagan fortress in Semgallia. Terweden saw a great deal of action between 1270 and 1290 in particular. It was a very solid stockade with high walls. Vertical support was supplied by massive tree trunks buried securely in the ground, around which a framework of interlocking timbers was raised. Careful cutting near the ends produces a neat and solid joint. The towers were roofed over with shingles above projecting beams.

And that was exactly what happened. Lithuanians were arriving all the time, so the crusader army had no choice but to fight its way through. Many were killed, and local enemy tribesmen cut down any cowards who fled:

> The master and his brothers put up a heroic defence until their horses were slain and even then they fought on foot and struck down many men before they were vanquished. Good Master Volkwin encouraged his brothers. Forty-eight made this stand and were attacked repeatedly. Finally, and with great difficulty, the Lithuanians killed them with long spears. God rest their souls. They, along with many other crusaders, departed this life in glory.

Almost all the Swordbrothers were wiped out at the battle of the Saule, the only survivors being those who had stayed behind on garrison duty. Demoralised and lacking in leadership, they appealed once again to the Teutonic Knights. They had little left with which to bargain, so in 1237 the survivors of the Swordbrothers were incorporated into the Teutonic Order and exchanged the mantles bearing a cross and a sword for ones bearing only the black cross. Herman Balk, the Master of Prussia, rode into Riga that summer and installed his own men as castle commanders and administrators in Livonia. The stone castles that the Swordbrothers had taken such pains to establish were now the property of the Teutonic Order. From that time onwards crusading affairs in Livonia would be in the hands of what was to become known as the Livonian Branch of the Teutonic Knights. On occasions they would still be referred to as the Swordbrothers, but in reality that entity had ceased to exist on the battlefield of the Saule in 1236, where the Order had made its last stand.

In 1238 the Teutonic Knights of Livonia concluded the Treaty of Stensby with the King of Denmark. Under this agreement northern maritime Estonia was handed back to Denmark in return for Danish support for expansion elsewhere, but the first result of the new policy was a defeat every bit as great as that inflicted at the Saule River on their predecessors. The Teutonic Knights of Livonia marched against the city of Novgorod. The campaign ended with the defeat of the crusaders by Alexander Nevsky in the famous 'battle on the ice' at Lake Peipus, immortalised forever in Eisenstein's film about the victor.

The multi-storey enclosed artillery tower of Treiden (Turaida), originally built during the 16th century and completely rebuilt as a restoration project.

The castles of Semgallia

During the decade that followed there was sporadic interference in the north from the Russians, but fortresses such as Weissenstein (Paide), built on land ceded to the Order by the king of Denmark following the Treaty of Stensby proved sufficient to contain the threat. This allowed the Order to concentrate on its southern borders and the area known as Semgallia. This was the strategic territory that lay immediately south of the Daugava and north of the Saule region of Samogitia. It was to be bitterly contested, because to pass through Semgallia was the quickest way for Lithuanians to raid settlements in Livonia and to reach the winter ice pack in the Gulf of Riga that made a bridge to Oesel (Saaremaa) Island.

There was another important reason for the brethren to pacify Semgallia, because pagan Semgallia and Samogitia kept the Livonian Branch of the Order physically separated from the Prussian Branch. The attempts to create a land bridge between them were to dominate much of the fighting that took place over the next century. The pagans were every bit as determined to keep them separate, and in 1245, for example, a Semgallian chief made a deep penetration into Teutonic territory. He even raided Wenden, the Order's headquarters, killing nine knights and forcing another to carry back with them the head of his commander. It was sacrificed in pagan ceremonies.

In 1252 the Prussian branch of the Teutonic Order made an important contribution to the unification attempts from the south when they established the castle of Memel (Klaipeda) at the northern tip of the Kurland Lagoon. Memel controlled entry from the Baltic Sea to the great river that was the gateway to Lithuania. It was known either as the Memel, the Neimen, the Neman or the Nemunas depending upon which territory it flowed through. The Teutonic Knights did not know it at the time, but the castle of Memel was to be the northernmost point ever occupied by the Prussian territories.

Meanwhile their Livonian comrades tried to extend their line to the south, and once again castle building played a major role in the strategy. As before the castles followed the line of rivers, and in many cases were established on native fortification sites. They were well defended, as shown in 1260 when the Samogitians attacked the Order's new foundation at Doblen (Dobele), but were forced to retire without causing a single fatality among the garrison. The Samogitians were also frustrated by the Order's ability to launch raids against them from inside the safety of castles, but castles did nothing to prevent another serious defeat for the Order at Durben in Kurland in 1260. The news of this incident sparked rebellions as far as the island of Oesel, and threatened to put the Order's efforts in Livonia back 20 years.

Part of the Order's fight back was mediated through a further strengthening of the castle line in Semgallia. In 1265 Mitau (Jelgava) was founded on the Aa River at the centre of a spider's web of intersecting waterways. There were certain political difficulties to clear up because the land on which Mitau was built belonged to the Archbishop of Riga, so papal permission had to be granted first. But the pagans still controlled the land routes, so sea and river transport became the only reliable means of supplying and reinforcing foundations like Mitau.

During the 1270s much of the fighting in Semgallia took place around the castle of Terweden (Tervete), a Semgallian earth and timber castle south-west of Mitau towards Samogitia. It was stormed by Walter von Nortecken in 1271, but in 1279 Terweden was retaken by the Semgallians and reverted to being a major bastion in the pagan defence system. On the opposing side Goldingen (Kuldiga) in Kurland now provided the best base for the Order's raids against the Semgallians. However, the loss of Terweden prompted the welcome arrival of German reinforcements who came to Riga to serve under the headstrong Livonian Marshal Gerhard of Katzenellenbogen, who met his end on a raid when he became separated from his men. The use of castles was a much preferable strategy, and in 1285/86 the incumbent Master Willekin demonstrated his organisational skills in the complex operations involved in building a castle. He first sent supplies by ship to Mitau and stored them in warehouses. When the ice had frozen thick enough for an army to march along the surface of the rivers he gathered his forces, took them from Riga to Mitau, loaded the supplies on to sleds and led the advance against Terweden. His plan was not to attack the castle immediately but to erect a fortress of his own nearby from which the garrison could harass the Semgallians. His men quickly constructed a timber and earth castle and called it Heiligenberg, the holy mountain, 'and its name later became famous', says the *Livonian Rhymed Chronicle*, which also tells us:

Now the garrisons of the castles of Heiligenberg and Terwerden are enemies, and their fighting caused many to suffer. There was a small depression between them, and so the garrisons could each quickly leave their respective castles and go down into the valley to do battle.

Master Willekin filled Heiligenberg with supplies, erected two stone-throwers on the walls, and left a garrison of 300 men equipped with crossbows to defend this isolated base. It proved a tempting challenge to the Semgallians. They sought aid from Samogitia and Heiligenberg, although only a temporary structure, was to see more siege activity over the next few years than most of the stone castles had experienced. The pagans' military technology had improved as a result of witnessing the crusaders' skills at siege warfare. While some warriors cut wood to built towers and catapults others moved protective barriers closer to the moat and threw in earth to fill it. On the eleventh day of the siege some Samogitians pushed their machines to the base of the castle's outer wall and began to dig under the foundations. But the resistance was fierce and the Samogitians were forced to flee. So precipitate was their flight that they abandoned those of their dead that they could not carry back for cremation, a practice normally unthinkable for them.

Faced by this desertion, the Semgallians inside Terwerden realised that their position was hopeless, so they burned the fortress and returned to the time-honoured alternative of raiding castles elsewhere as soon as they had recovered their strength. Both Riga and Uexkull suffered in this way. The two castles held out, but a relieving force to Uexkull from the Order was surprised and cut to pieces. Many in the Livonian

Although very little is left at the site of the castle of Kremon (Krimulda), this corner of the interior shows the use made of three different building materials. On the ground we see undressed stone boulder used for foundations. The walls are made from a combination of red brick and dressed stone.

The southern side of Segewold (Sigulda) castle, superbly and sensitively restored to give a fine impression of a stone crusader castle. The tower on the left covers the gatehouse, while the building on the right is the gable end of the convent building of the Swordbrothers.

Order's high command perished at Uexkull, so reinforcements were sent from Prussia under the newly elected Livonian Master Cuno of Hattstein. He sailed round from Memel and made his way upriver to Goldingen. The proof that the sea and river route was safe put great heart into the Livonian brethren, as did his subsequent expedition into Semgallia.

The pagans hit back defiantly by crossing the Daugava and raiding north, but it was an unwise move because Master Cuno saw his chance of destroying Semgallia while its defenders were elsewhere. So he drove quickly and more deeply than ever into Semgallia. The tactic was a tremendous success and Semgallian resistance collapsed. With the capture of Semgallia the conquest of Livonia begun by Bishop Albert nine decades earlier was effectively completed.

The Teutonic Knights of Livonia did not realise it at the time, but the overthrow of pagan Semgallia in 1290 was the last permanent conquest in their history. To the south lay the pagan Lithuanian territory of Samogitia that kept them so tantalisingly separate from their Prussian brethren, but between Semgallia and Samogitia there now ran a border that was to be often challenged but never permanently changed. It is still there as the modern frontier between Latvia and Lithuania, and marks the place where the Livonian Branch of the Teutonic Knights finally fought itself to a standstill.

New castles and new challenges

Once the Semgallians had been subdued during the 1290s the biggest threat to the Order's plans to make Livonia into another Prussia came from a very different direction, but once again the use of castles was to be a decisive factor.

By the end of the 13th century the manner in which the first 100 years of crusading had been conducted meant that the map of Livonia was a complex patchwork of territories, each defended by its own castles. There were first of all the Order's own lands, inherited from the Swordbrothers and augmented since by treaty and conquest. The Archbishop of Riga, the Bishop of Dorpat and the Bishop of Oesel-Wiek were independent prelates, but the Bishop of Kurland was dependent on the Teutonic Knights.

Yet it was the city of Riga, semi-independent and allied with the growing Hanseatic League, that provided the new challenge of the 14th century. Much of the economic output from the Order's castles and estates was channelled through Riga and made it one of the largest cities in northern Europe. Prussia had nothing to compare with Riga, which was the focal point for trade in grain, furs, wax and animals. It was far from being an ice-free port, but merchants cheerfully sailed up the Daugava (Dvina) in summer and slid up it in winter. As Riga attracted so much passing traffic its hostelries, shops and craftsmen exuded wealth, and its skyline sported the grand towers and spires of numerous fine churches, many of which remain to this day.

One result of Riga's prosperity was the existence of a three-cornered rivalry between the archbishop in his cathedral, the Order in the former Swordbrothers' castle of St George and the industrious citizens. The Rigans never saw much of the Livonian brethren unless they were heading off to war or returning victorious, but they were always wary of them and took appropriate precautions. So the rich burghers trained as knights and could easily afford to recruit mercenaries. They also built a wall round the city – just in case.

Matters came to a head in 1297 when the very mundane matter of flood control on the Daugava provoked the first major clash between the two sides. Successive flooding and freezing had often created enormous ice floes that nearly topped the city walls. To deal with the problem the citizens began a building programme to divert the floods. The scheme made use of an island in the Daugava, so a bridge was built with a movable centre span that could be lifted to allow river traffic to pass through. The bridge proved to be such an asset to the city that when the flood defences were finished the council decided to make it a permanent feature. It was this that caused alarm in the Order's cloisters. A bridge could allow any rebellious citizens to close off the river against the Order's troops, so the Teutonic Knights simply destroyed it under cover of darkness.

The subsequent protest delivered to St George's produced nothing but the contemptuous reply that anything the Rigans could build in ten days the Order would tear down in half a day. The defiant citizens ignored the threat and rebuilt their bridge, so the Order went to war on its own doorstep in the dramatic fashion described in the later section on operational history. Peace talks held over the Christmas period ended in fisticuffs, and soon the third member of the Riga triangle became involved. The archbishop had been absent during the initial squabbles over the bridge, and on his return he had immediately fled. He now found himself besieged by the brethren in one of his castles. They captured him and sent him as a prisoner to Wenden. The repercusions of the conflict were felt throughout Livonia. For example, the Bishop of Oesel-Wiek was so alarmed that he mobilised an army in case the dispute spread to his territories. News crossed the border into Lithuania, and, with a possible civil war looming, the Lithuanians realised their moral obligation to make things just that little bit worse!

The raid was the first Lithuanian invasion of Livonia for a decade, and it was intended to help the citizens of Riga against the Order. At first the incursion seemed to have saved Riga, but all it did in the long run was to provoke an intervention from the Teutonic Knights of Prussia. The climax was a pitched battle between the Teutonic Order and an allied army of the citizens of Riga and Lithuania. The Order was victorious, and in the resulting peace settlement the Archbishop of Riga was set free and restored to all his properties except for his castles. As for Riga, a 'peace-line' was drawn:

between the city and the property of the Order, the Order shall build at its cost a thick wall nine feet high without bothering the streets or open spaces of the city … and the brothers can live only in that area, and they may have only one rear door four feet wide and six high through which one man can go to buy or obtain food for the brothers. Besides the gate that the brothers had in the city wall before the quarrel began, they cannot have any other, not even in the church.

The fortifications of Riga come back into the story in 1330. Fighting broke out anew, and once again the citizens sought help from a Lithuanian army. But while the Lithuanians were busy raiding elsewhere the Teutonic Knights besieged Riga and brought about its surrender by starvation. The capitulation treaty of 30 March 1330 required the citizens to grant the Order a site where they might build a new castle as a replacement for St George's. The result was the building of Riga castle, which still stands on the same site on the banks of the Daugava, although it has since been considerably rebuilt. It was by no means a harsh settlement – the cities of Prussia had submitted to much worse, but the Rigans had valued their independence and bitterly regretted its loss.

The haughty Teutonic Knights tore a gap of 50ft in the city walls for their victory parade to demonstrate the extent to which they had triumphed.

But while the Livonian Branch flourished the Teutonic Knights of Prussia entered into a long but serious decline. The union of Poland and Lithuania in 1386 under the newly baptised King Wladislaw Jagiello meant that the fiction of a Lithuanian Crusade could no longer be sustained. It also placed a formidably strong foe on the Order's frontier in the shape of Catholic Poland. In 1410 the Teutonic Knights of Prussia were heavily defeated at the battle of Tannenberg/Grunwald, and then the humiliating Second Treaty of Torun in 1466 ceded to Poland the western part of its Prussian domains. By the early 1520s the spread of the Reformation was already undermining the Order in its traditional recruiting grounds. In 1525 the last Grand Master Albrecht von Hohenzollern secularised the Order and established the Duchy of Prussia as a fief of the Polish crown.

At first the Livonian Branch weathered the storm and even expanded northwards, well away from the troubles in Prussia. In 1434 the Livonian Order took advantage of the absence in Rome of the Bishop of Oesel-Wiek to take over his territories. Several castles changed hands from one side to the other. For example, the castles of Hapsal (Haapsalu) and Arensburg (Kuressaare) were captured by the order, only to be lost and then attacked again in 1448. But from the time of the Treaty of Torun in 1466 onwards the Livonian Order began to look terribly isolated. Ivan III's conquest of Novgorod brought Muscovite power much closer to Livonia's borders, but a breathing space was gained when Muscovite forces were defeated by Master Walter von Plettenburg in 1501 and 1502.

When Pskov was subjugated in 1510 Muscovy became Estonia's immediate neighbour. Worse was to come. We noted above that Albrecht von Hohenzollern had secularised the Teutonic Order in Prussia and had accepted a Polish dukedom. The Livonian Order, now the sole representatives of the Teutonic Knights on the Baltic, saw this as a betrayal of all they stood for. Albrecht, for his part, feared that the Livonian Order might try and take his new duchy from him, so when the Livonian Order faced the new threat from Muscovy Albrecht did not support them. Turning away from their traditional friends, the Livonian Order looked elsewhere for allies. In 1551 a defence treaty was signed in Vilnius by Gotthard Kettler, the last Master of the Livonian Order, and the Polish Chancellor Nicholas Radziwill. In accordance with the treaty Poland/Lithuania promised to supply the Order with troops for its wars against Muscovy. In return the Livonian Order loaned some frontier areas and castles to Poland/Lithuania for a temporary period. For example, Bauske (Bauska) castle was handed over to the representative of the Polish king in December 1559.

Such support was sorely needed, because the Livonian Order now had a new Muscovite enemy in the person of the famous Ivan the Terrible, who entered Livonia in 1558 with an impressive artillery train in tow. Castle after castle in northern Estonia fell without a shot being fired. Narva surrendered in May and Dorpat (Tartu) in July. The recapture of Wesenburg (Rakvere) in October was but a temporary remission, and on 2 August 1560 the Livonian Order made its last stand at the battle of Ermes.

Ermes was not a glorious defeat, but a short bloody struggle in a dark forest in an obscure corner of northern Latvia. With a force consisting of a few hundred members of the Order and 500 auxiliaries, Philipp Schall von Bell boldly but unwisely took on a much larger Muscovite army. So confident was he of victory that he did not wait to join up with his Lithuanian allies who were waiting to the south. Half the Order's army was killed or captured, while Schall von Bell was dragged to Moscow and executed. His body was exposed in the street. The Livonian Order had perished, so the last Master of Livonia, Gotthard Kettler, secularised the Order and took the title of the Duke of Kurland. It was the end of an era.

Chronology

The magnificent gatehouse tower of Segewold (Sigulda), one of the finest surviving ruins in Latvia.

1184	Meinhard establishes the first mission in Livonia
1185	Uexkull (Ilkskile) castle is built
1190	The founding of the Teutonic Order in the Holy Land
1198	First battle between German crusaders and native Livonians; Bishop Albert takes over the mission
1204	Founding of the Swordbrothers
1205	First battle involving the Swordbrothers
1208	Founding of castles of Segewold (Sigulda) and Wenden (Cesis)
1211	Advance by Swordbrothers into Estonia – siege of Fellin (Viljandi)
1222	Partition of Estonia
1229	Death of Bishop Albert
1236	Battle of the Saule. The Swordbrothers are heavily defeated.
1237	The Sword Brothers of Livonia are absorbed by the Teutonic Order
1242	The Teutonic Order is defeated by Alexander Nevsky at Lake Peipus (the battle on the ice)
1260	Defeat of Livonian Order at the battle of Durben
1290	Conquest of Semgallia
1297	First clash between the Teutonic Order and the citizens of Riga
1330	Building of Riga castle
1386	Wladyslaw Jagiello is baptized and becomes King of Poland
1410	The battle of Tannenberg/Grunwald – defeat of the Teutonic Order
1411	First Treaty of Thorn (Torun)
1434	The Livonian Order captures castles from the Bishop of Oesel-Wiek
1466	Second Treaty of Thorn (Torun)
1525	Secularisation of the Teutonic Order in Prussia
1551	Treaty of Vilnius
1558	Ivan the Terrible invades Livonia
1560	Last stand of the Livonian Order at the battle of Ermes

The former chapel of St George's castle, Riga, the first castle of the Order of Swordbrothers in the future capital of Latvia. It is now a museum, which has preserved this important site from the earliest days of crusader activity in Livonia.

Design features of the crusader castles

The first wooden castles

When the first crusaders arrived in Livonia to build their stone castles they discovered a well-established local tradition of building fortresses in wood. In many cases this technique was adopted as an immediate measure for securing conquered areas before stone castles could be built. Also, just as in Prussia, timber provided a ready means of establishing a temporary strongpoint while on campaign.

Local allies of the crusaders also operated out of their own timber forts in support of the German knights. An excellent example of this practice is the chief known as Caupo, mentioned by name in Henry of Livonia's chronicle, who ruled the Livs of the Livonian Aa River (now the Gauja River) north of Riga. His headquarters was on the banks of the Aa at the site now known as Turaida. The castle was a most impressive timber structure built either in the second half of the 11th century or at the latest at the turn of the 12th century. The timber fortress extended to the very edge of the plateau. It was later replaced by the Order's castle of Treiden, which covered a smaller area. The Turaida Livs threw up a defensive bank almost 20ft wide, and the fortifications included a wall of horizontal logs supported by vertical posts.

Few artefacts have been unearthed from the original Turaida site, but fortunately a nearby archaeological excavation has added greatly to our knowledge of timber-working in Latvia. This was technology that was also

The lake fortress of Araisu, which shows the methods of timber construction used in the hillforts of the pagan Livonians.

incorporated into the wooden parts of the stone crusader castles. The site is the remarkable lake fortress of Araisu, where archaeological investigations have shed light on the methods of timber construction used in the 9th to 10th centuries by the Latgallians, the largest ancient Latvian tribe. The remains of 145 wooden houses, ancillary buildings and defensive structures have been uncovered. Part of the site has been rebuilt.

Latvian historians have applied similar building principles to create a hypothetical reconstruction of the original Turaida castle. The result is a very solid stockade with high walls. Vertical support is supplied by massive tree trunks buried securely in the ground, around which a framework of interlocking timbers is raised. Careful cutting near the ends produces a neat and solid joint rather like the traditional log cabin of the American West. The towers are roofed over with shingles above projecting beams. The timber castles of Terweden and Heiligenberg that figure so strongly in the historical narrative above would have been very similar.

The design and construction of the stone castles

We know from Henry of Livonia that the basic structure of the first stone castle in Livonia was stones held together by mortar. In a very revealing passage he tells us how this fact was unknown to the pagans, who presumed that the stones were simply piled one on top of another. It was only when they tried to pull the walls down using ships' ropes that they realised that the stones were bonded together.

The simplest method of timber wall construction, as shown by a model in the Vytautas the Great Military Museum in Kaunas, Lithuania.

The earliest stone castles were not elaborate affairs. The builders first took advantage of whatever natural defensive features the site possessed. These were often considerable, because the pagan tribes had used many of the sites before. Water defences were common, and the castles were often located upon a promontory left by the confluence of two rivers. Kokenhusen (Koknese) provides an excellent example, although the modern rise in the water level of the Daugava has obscured the effect.

Thick upright stone walls protected by ditches formed the main defences. There were few provisions for flanking fire, and the stone was always augmented by timber. We may therefore understand the earliest castles as being simple stone blockhouses in the form of a single tower with an adjoining wall or just a walled enclosure with integral buildings. Holm (Salaspils) on the Daugava provides an early example of a simple walled area. It was the second castle to be associated with Bishop Meinhard, and dates from about 1186. Excavations have revealed a design of an almost perfect square of stone walls with a tower at one corner. It was protected on three sides by a ditch, and on the fourth by the waters of the Daugava. Holm, under its later name Kirkholm, was the site of a celebrated battle in the 17th century. There is nothing left of the castle today.

Holm provides the first example of a tower being incorporated into the wall. At Arensburg (Kuressaare) on Oesel (Saaremaa) Island the

The developed form of convent courtyard – Ronneburg (Rauna) 1500
This plate shows the final developed form of inner convent courtyard in the years prior to the dissolution of the Livonian Branch of the Teutonic Knights. Ronneburg (Rauna) is in northern Latvia, and this reconstruction is based on archaeological plans and reconstructions. By the 16th century a stone outer wall containing five towers enclosed the rectangular inner courtyard of the Order's convent. The roof design at Ronneburg is interesting. The overall surface area of the convent was retained and expansion was carried out in an upward direction. The buildings that make up the four walls of the convent were increased in height and the roofs now only sloped inwards. The result was a structure of forbidding solidity when viewed from an attacker's perspective. This is a similar development to the rebuilding that took place at Hapsal (Haapsalu) in Estonia, which is illustrated elsewhere in this book. Most reconstructions show that the main entrance to Ronneburg was via an underground passage, making it very difficult to capture. The large chapel may also be noted. In the courtyard there are stables and tents.

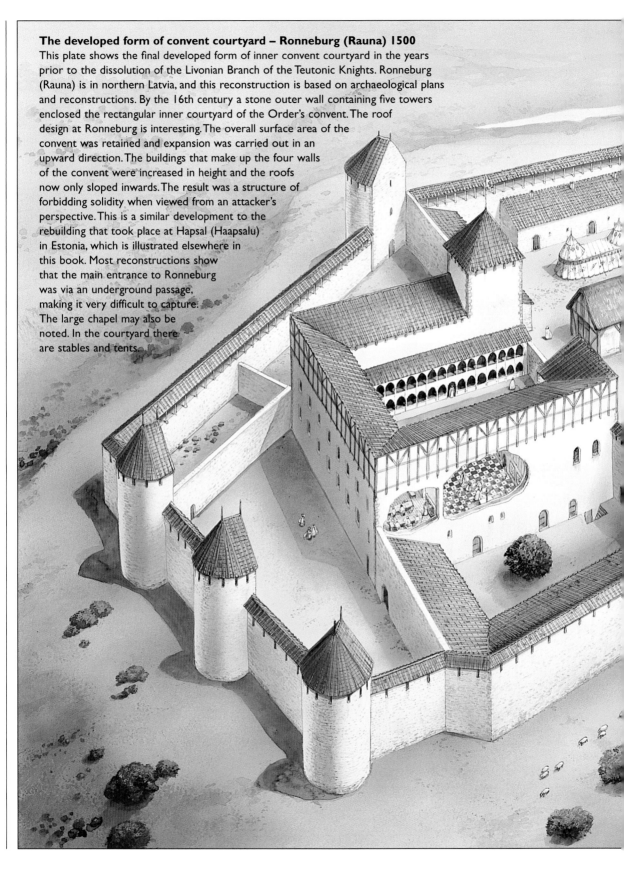

ABOVE The south face of the ruins of Wenden (Cesis), the headquarters of the Swordbrothers and for many years the headquarters of the Livonian Branch of the Teutonic Knights. On the left is the West Tower, which has a square cross section in its lower half and a circular artillery tower on top. On the right is the so-called 'Lange Hermann' tower.

tower also lay at one of the corners. It was much larger than Holm, and is described in detail below. Lonely Wolkenburg (Makonkalns) was perhaps the simplest design of all, and probably consisted of a round tower within a wall on a mound.

The corner tower provided the basis for the next development in castle construction. This was the creation of a very solid rectangular courtyard. It became the characteristic model of the 'fortified monastery' or 'Convent of the Knights' that was to be found both in Prussia and Livonia. The identical style may be seen in castles that were owned by the bishops as well as the Order's own properties. The walls of the convent courtyard were two- or three-storey buildings covered over with steeply pitched roofs. Inside would be all the requirements for living the joint life of knight and friar: a chapel, refectory, storage areas, living quarters, armouries and the like. In the basic model at least one formidable corner tower would play the role of a keep to provide a last refuge in war. The isolated sewage tower, the remarkable latrine block that was such as feature of all Teutonic Order castles in Prussia, is not found as frequently in Livonia.

As the roles required of a castle increased so the overall layout of the castle would expand to meet these needs. Other towers might be added, or the quadrangle might be duplicated to produce a rectangle. The design of the convent at Ronneburg (Rauna) is interesting in this regard because it represents a further development in architectural style, whereby the overall surface area of the convent was retained and expansion was carried out in an upward direction. The buildings that make up the four walls of the convent were increased in height and the roofs now only sloped inwards. The result was a structure of forbidding solidity when viewed from an attacker's perspective.

This process of converting a convent courtyard of *c*. 1400 to the new and stronger form of *c*. 1500 is illustrated by the two accompanying drawings that

RIGHT The great round North Tower of Wenden (Cesis), viewed from the ravine that protects the castle.

refer to Hapsal (Haapsalu) castle (see page 32). In the uppermost picture we see a reconstruction of the convent of 1400. There are two prominent square towers across the courtyard from the chapel complex to which they are joined by a comparatively low wall. By 1500 all the walls have been raised to the level of the tops of the towers, and the pitched roofs have been replaced by roofs that slope towards the centre of the courtyard. The modest tower in the centre of the wall has grown to become a tall round tower. From the outside these sheer walls must have looked insurmountable. A similar but more complex arrangement of walls and towers may be noted in the illustrations included here of Arensburg (Kuressaare).

Another development was to enclose the courtyard complex within an outer wall. This would be much lower than the convent walls and would provide an additional outer line of defence enclosing an outer bailey. Towers would often be included in such a wall. Excavations at Ronneberg (Rauna) castle give an excellent illustration of this style. By the 16th century at Ronneberg a stone outer wall containing five towers enclosed the rectangular inner courtyard. At Fellin (Viljandi) the entire convent courtyard, including its chapel, is neatly enclosed within the stone outer walls that reach to the very edge of the rocky plateau on which it is built. In other examples the contrast between the inner courtyard area and the outer bailey is more marked as it is dependent upon geographical features. So the courtyard at Kokenhusen (Koknese) was limited by the edges of the triangular patch of land at the top of cliffs, while the outer bailey spread down the slope. Wolmar (Valmiera) was very similar but of a more complex shape. At Fellin the outer bailey then grew to enclose the town inside its encircling arms of walls and towers. The same happened at Kokenhusen, as shown by a drawing made in 1625, but at Segewold (Sigulda) and Treiden (Turaida) the limits of the rocky plateau defined the castle's entire shape.

The other defining factor in determining a castle's layout was its relative importance in the defensive system. So Kremon (Krimulda) was a modest stone structure built on a rocky plateau across the Aa (Gauja) River from Segewold. Its shape was an irregular hexagon of stone walls with a tower in the northern corner and other buildings in the southern corner. Otherwise there is nothing at Kremon of the developed convent style. Little is left of Kremon nowadays, but an examination of the ruins shows the utilisation of three types of building material in its construction. Massive natural boulders are used for the foundations of the walls, which are finished using dressed stone and some red brick.

By contrast, mighty Wenden (Cesis) expanded from a basic courtyard model to the massive complex described below. Segewold (Sigulda) lies in between Kremon and Wenden in size, but like Kremon it utilises every inch of space available on its rocky plateau. The overall shape is therefore highly irregular, being determined only by the topography of its ground plan. The main entrance to Segewold, on its southern side, has been superbly and sensitively restored to give a stunning

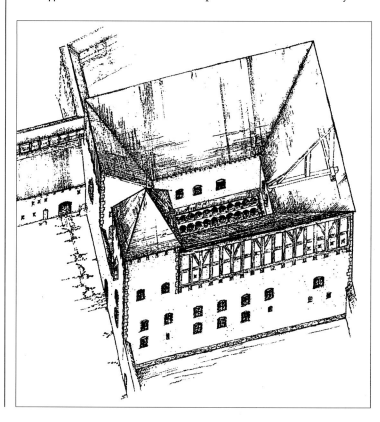

The convent building of Ronneberg (Rauna), showing the rectangular inner courtyard. The roof design at Ronneburg is interesting because apart from the four-sided corner tower the roofs slope inwards towards the courtyard rather than being pitched. Note the use of timber in the upper sections of the wall.

The impact of artillery on Livonian castle design – Treiden (Turaida) castle 1560

The most important developments in castle design came about as a result of the need to provide suitable structures in which cannon could be mounted. One result, a multi-storey artillery tower, is shown here at the castle of Treiden (Turaida). Treiden was unique in Latvia in that stone provided little more than the foundations. The remainder of the superstructure was made from red bricks, thus producing an edifice that resembled the Teutonic Order's castles in Prussia. The artillery tower is of semicircular cross section and forms an integral part of the wall. The armaments include a large-scale arquebus, breech-loading cannon and a large cannon on a gun carriage.

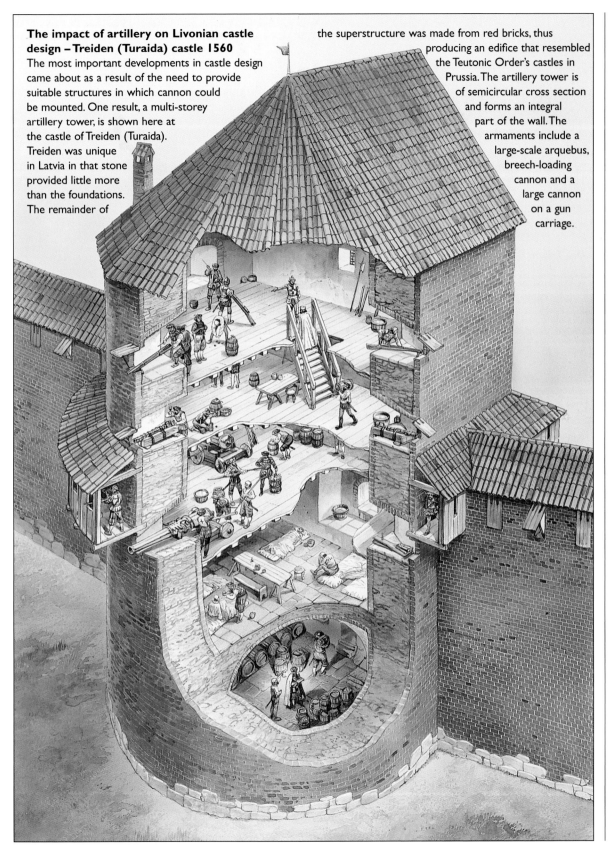

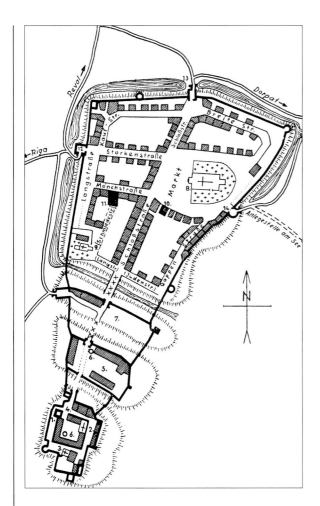

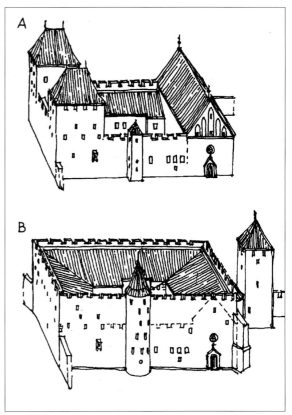

impression of this aspect of a Livonian castle. Inside the courtyard the buildings of the convent, which make use of the outer wall because of lack of space, are all in a picturesque ruined state.

In almost every case the predominant building material used in the crusader castles was locally quarried stone, usually dolomite, augmented by red brick. In most cases the brick was used for the finer details of windows and the like. In this context Treiden (Turaida) is unique in Latvia in that stone provided little more than the foundations. The remainder of the superstructure was made from red bricks, thus producing an edifice that resembled the Teutonic Order's castles in Prussia. Treiden was built on the site of the pagan timber fortress described above. It is generally agreed that the original 13th-century castle consisted of a long, narrow and irregularly walled enclosure with a chapel built into the wall, but the most distinctive feature of Treiden was its huge chimney-like red-brick tower with a conical roof. This has been reconstructed and is the most striking feature of the site today. The walls and the top of the tower had battlements. In later years these walls grew to resemble the conventional convent buildings, while a later addition was a multi-storey artillery tower of semicircular cross section.

Different responses to the introduction of artillery may be noted at several other sites. Some castle towers were lowered to provide better elevation for shooting over a moat, and were also made thicker and much more solid to resist bombardment. There are examples of both practices at Wenden (Cesis). At Arensburg (Kuressaare) there is an interesting 16th-century round artillery tower. The final addition that many castles now possess was provided in the years following the secularisation of the Livonian Order. This was the creation of huge encircling angle bastions during the 17th century. Bauske (Bauska) and Arensburg (Kuressaare) show excellent examples built from earth. Riga's stone

bastions were created at this time but have since disappeared. A map of Wolmar (Valmiera) dating from 1688 shows how the bastions enclose the medieval structures without altering them in any appreciable way.

ABOVE LEFT Detail of an ornamented doorway from the courtyard to the convent building at Doblen.

ABOVE RIGHT The reconstructed cylindrical tower of Treiden (Turaida). Unlike other Livonian castles, Treiden was built out of red brick. This tower is the most spectacular edifice in the modern reconstruction.

Castle maintenance and decoration

If neglected or abandoned a castle site could deteriorate rapidly, as Bishop Albert found when he inspected Kokenhusen (Koknese):

> Thereupon with all the pilgrims and his army, he went off to Kokenhusen. Finding the mountain deserted and, because of the filthiness of the former inhabitants, full of snakes and worms, he ordered and asked that it be cleansed and renovated, and had it strongly fortified. He built a very strong fort there and left knights, ballistarii (torsion catapults) and his household to take care of it.

Further consequences of the lack of hygiene in a castle were demonstrated when plague broke out in Latvia and decimated the loyal natives. The disease spread most rapidly among those guarding the forts and drinking impure water.

Inside the castles the Teutonic Knights allowed an artistic expression that could not be risked on the purely functional exteriors of their fortresses. Wenden contains attractive brick ceiling vaulting for example, but this was by no means a universal practice. Segewold uses stone for decoration.

Perspective drawing of Kokenhusen (Koknese) from 1625, showing how the space on the top of the plateau was utilised.

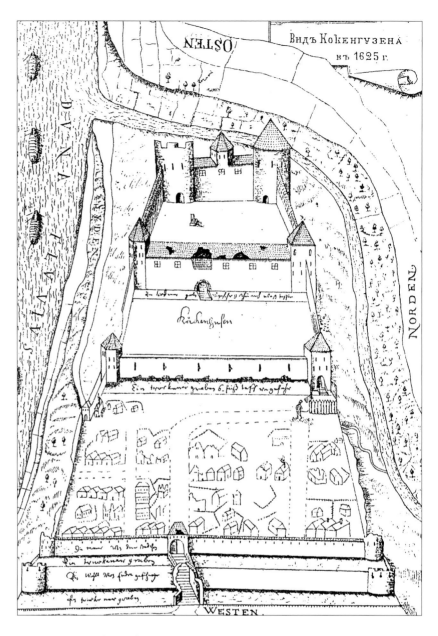

At Wenden the Refectory consisted of a cross-vaulted room with three octagonal piers, decorated with portraits of past masters. The ornate chapel was destroyed when the castle was blown up in defiance of Ivan the Terrible, but the late 15th-century brick vaulting inside the western tower still survives. It was originally covered in blue glazing. Riga was also richly decorated inside, with a statue of the Virgin and Child over one of the gates. Just as in Prussia, devotion to the Virgin ensured that her image was the most frequently seen motif in castle decoration.

The crusader castles as a defensive system

Control by castles

As indicated above, the control of Livonia was exercised through the crusader castles, but the means of control differed according to which frontier was being defended. The eastern frontier had to cope with the large but usually well publicised invasions launched from either Russia or Lithuania every few decades. The castles there were few in number and set back from the border. The southern frontier presented an entirely different problem. The main threat to security here came from more numerous but smaller-scale raids launched from Samogitia or by the unconverted pagans in Semgallia. The raiders followed the usual tactical pattern of the region, which was to use surprise, seize women and children as slaves and escape as soon as possible with their booty. To some extent this process played into the Order's hands, because converted tribes usually stayed loyal out of fear of being raided.

The Swordbrothers were the great teachers of the Teutonic Knights in matters of strategic defence. Two decades before the Prussian crusade began the doomed Swordbrothers had worked out the best methods for converting and conquering a pagan land. Not only had they discovered that the depths of winter were the best times for campaigning, they had also demonstrated a successful holding strategy based on the setting up of chains of castles along the lines of rivers. So, for example, the Daugava castles sheltered the tribes to the north of the river.

Lennewarden (Lielvarde) castle lies on the Daugava a few miles upstream from Ikskile. Here we see a small corner tower of the remains of the convent building.

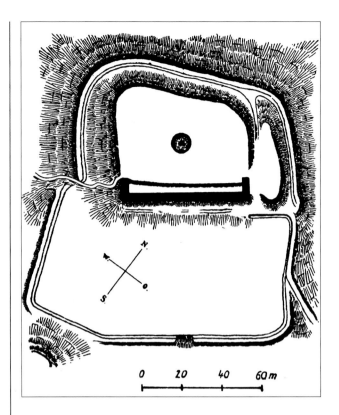

Plan of Wolkenburg. Lonely Wolkenburg (Makonkalns) was perhaps the simplest castle design of all, consisting of a round tower within a wall on a mound on the shore of Lake Razna in Lettgallia (Latgale).

To the west castles such as Mitau and Mesoten (Mezotne) protected communications into Kurland, where the great castle of Goldingen (Kuldiga) anchored a further string of castles.

The crusader castles of Livonia were no Maginot Line. No castle garrison ever managed to block an attack, but as raiders wanted booty rather than battle a direct assault was a rare event. The castles acted instead as military bases from where the brothers could mount patrols against raids and then launch counter-offensives of their own. A longer-term strategy then developed whereby the interior could be opened up to convert or conquer the tribes, again under the protection of fortified places.

The ideal to which the Order aspired was that castles should not be built further apart than the distance that their patrols could watch effectively. But in practice the castles around the heartland of Livonia were built quite close together, while the further from the settlements one went the more widely separated the castles became. Between Dünamünde and Uexkull there were four castles within a space of just over 30 miles. Lennewarden (Lielvarde) was 12 miles upstream. Ascheraden lay 21 miles further on and Kokenhusen (Koknese) was another 18 miles distant. From that point distances increased greatly. Gerzike (Jersika) was 50 miles away, and Dünaburg (Daugavpils) lay another 44 miles upstream. Finally lonely Wolkenburg (Makonkalns) lay isolated 62 miles into the interior on the shore of Lake Razna in Lettgallia (Latgale).

Rivers and castles

The selection of places at which to site the castles was not entirely due to the Swordbrothers' military genius. In many cases they simply took over existing sites that had long been appreciated for their defensive value by the peoples the crusaders conquered. This is hardly surprising, given the importance of the rivers to Livonia. The Daugava (Dvina), for example, was one of the most important trade and transport routes in Eastern Europe and had been used as such since the Stone Age. The upper reaches of the Daugava are in close proximity to the upper courses of three other rivers – the Volga, giving passageway to the Caspian Sea, the Dneiper, which flows to the Black Sea, and the Lovar, which allows access to the Gulf of Finland in the Baltic. Portages made it fairly easy to cross from one river to another. Contact between the Daugava and the Dnieper took place through at least four portages.

As the Daugava nowadays has been radically controlled by dams and hydroelectric schemes it is difficult to appreciate that at the time of the Teutonic Knights the greatest river in Latvia was notorious for the large number of rapids along its 640-mile stretch. Over 100 rapids were identified and known. The ones lowest down the river were regarded as the most dangerous because they were caused by rock thresholds that spanned the entire river. Well-fortified pagan hillforts had long been located at these points so that river traffic could be firmly controlled from the banks. One hillfort, Daugmale, has recently been excavated to reveal an extensive complex consisting of a wooden castle with an adjacent early town, a harbour and two burial places.

It was therefore to be expected that when the crusaders arrived the same sites would begin to sprout stone castles. When Bishop Meinhard built Latvia's

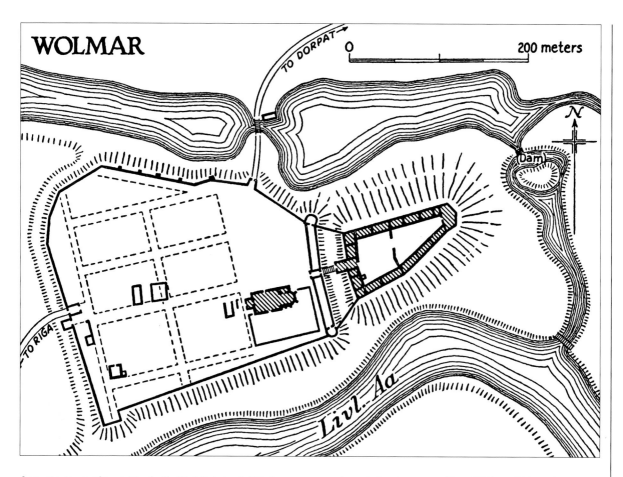

WOLMAR

TO DORPAT→

0   200 meters

Dam

TO RIGA

Livl-Aa

first stone castle at Uexkull (Ikskile) in 1185 he was merely reinforcing a practice that had existed for centuries. The building of Lennewarden (Leilvarde) a few miles upstream in 1205 was begun on top of the smouldering ruins of a Liv fortress. Similarly, the later fortresses of the Order on the islands of Estonia followed established settlements. Five pagan fortified strongholds were founded on the islands of Oesel (Saaremaa) and Mohn (Muhu) in the 12th and beginning of the 13th century.

In addition to their role as frontier posts the castles also provided a rallying point for the native militia units drawn from loyal converts, who would be led into battle by a small force of mounted Teutonic Knights. When a raiding party was spotted, often by plumes of smoke from burning villages, the men of the militia hurried to the castle while their families sought shelter in the forests or in local stockades. The patrols watched for the raiders' return and, as they were able to move more quickly than raiders laden with booty, they would usually destroy them. It was a process that discouraged repeated incursions, and the castles played a vital role by providing the secure bases that were necessary.

The defence of individual castles

When it came to individual defence, the Livonian castles provided a challenge to an attacker from the moment he approached. A succession of walls and ditches surrounded the final entrance to a castle, which was itself constructed so that an attacker could be observed at every stage. When an enemy finally launched an attack, he was faced with sheer stone walls and massive gates. The developed form of the convent courtyard was particularly intimidating. Arensburg (Kuressaare) provides a striking example of a high, smooth stone surface that is impossible to scale because it rises perpendicularly from the

Plan of Wolmar (Valmiera), a typical 'castle on a promontory' design in northern Latvia, enclosing the town.

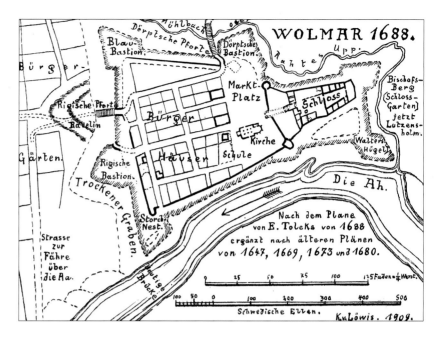

Map of Wolmar (Valmiera) in 1688. The map shows how the bastions enclosed the medieval structures without altering them in any appreciable way.

ground. The main gate to the convent courtyard was always defended from inside a formidable gatehouse behind a drawbridge. Arensburg also provides the threatening sight of a dark narrow passage as its entrance, across which a portcullis was suspended.

If the courtyard was lost, the garrison could withdraw into the tower and keep assailants at bay with crossbows. In Prussia the detached sewage tower that is found at most sites could provide a last line of defence. This feature was much less common in Livonia. Finally, as the castles had strong foundations it would take an attacker many days of effort to use the alternative approach of tunnelling under such a strong structure and undermining it. The location of other castles nearby was also a disincentive to lengthy mining operations.

In addition to the walls and towers themselves, a garrison armed with and skilled at using various anti-personnel weapons defended the Livonian castles. Long before gunpowder weapons were available the crusader castle defensive system depended upon the combination of timber and stone from which protruded numerous crossbows, the brothers' favourite weapons. Their reliance on the crossbow is best illustrated by an incident during the 1279 operation at Terweden (Tervete). A German archer was spared his life when the outworks were overrun because he agreed to teach the pagans the use of the crossbow:

> There was a knave there named Berthold, and the Semgallians spared him because he was an archer ... The Semgallians soon found plenty of crossbows and arrows in the outer works of the castle. This pleased them greatly and they quickly gathered them all together. The evil Christian selected and assembled as many men to be archers as there were crossbows and gave instructions to whomever did not know how to draw and fire.

This resulted in the inner tower becoming untenable, so the Knights set fire to it and sallied out in a suicidal attack.

Cannon came on to the scene towards the end of the 14th century, but at this stage in history siege guns were by no means as effective as they would be a century later because of the difficulties of transportation. The need to drag heavy siege guns along almost non-existent roads or barge them along rivers meant that in several actions the artillery was simply left behind.

Representative crusader castles of Livonia

The following castles illustrate the developments in Livonian fortification technology from the time of the founding of Uexkull to the final modifications applied to Riga castle within a few years of the dissolution of the Livonian Branch of the Teutonic Order.

Uexkull (Ikskile)

The remains of Latvia's first castle of the 1180s have been unintentionally preserved from further decay by their isolation on an island in the middle of the Daugava as the result of a rise in the water level following dam building. Uexkull appears to have consisted of a very simple set of interconnected buildings that anticipated the future courtyard model. The three main buildings had a stone wall in front of them enclosing a yard. The central building, although tower-like, lacked the pure defensive aspect of the tower at Arensburg described below.

St George's in Riga

One of the most important early sites in Latvia was the castle of the Swordbrothers in Riga, otherwise known as St George's. All that remains now is the building that was once the castle chapel. The shape of St George's chapel is an elongated rectangle, and the apse is the oldest surviving part. When the castle was built the constant warfare meant that local dolomite could not be quarried, so stone was shipped in from Germany while bricks were produced locally. St George's was extended when the Teutonic Knights took over from the Swordbrothers, and survived until its demolition by the citizens in the incident of 1297 described above. In 1330 the new Riga castle was built on the site of the old hospital of the Order, which had stood there since 1220, so the hospital was moved to St George's and renamed the Convent of the Holy Spirit. St George's survival in the historic heart of old Riga has been almost miraculous. It has served as a storehouse in the past, but now houses a museum. The accompanying plan shows how the surviving chapel once completed the rectangle of courtyard buildings indicated by dotted lines.

Plan of St George's in Riga. All that remains now is the building that was once the castle chapel, the shape of which is an elongated rectangle. The apse is the oldest surviving part. St George's was extended when the Teutonic Knights took over from the Swordbrothers and lasted until its demolition by the citizens in the incident of 1297. The plan shows how the surviving chapel once completed the rectangle of courtyard buildings indicated by dotted lines.

Arensburg (Kuressaare)

One of the most dramatic examples of a Livonian castle lies on the southern coast of the Estonian island of Oesel (Saaremaa). Unlike most other examples, the stretch of water that Arensburg covered was not a river but the sea of the Gulf of Riga; however, in the depths of winter even the sea froze over.

The first stone castle on the site replaced an original timber structure believed to date from the 11th century. That was destroyed by fire in one of the encounters between the Swordbrothers and the Oeselians, as evidenced by charred timbers. The actual incident probably took place when the

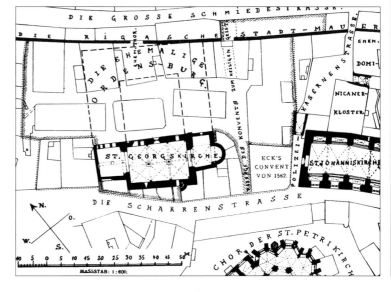

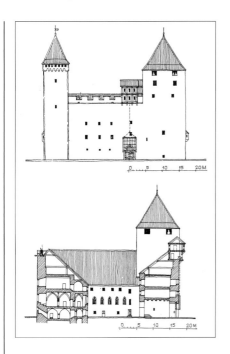

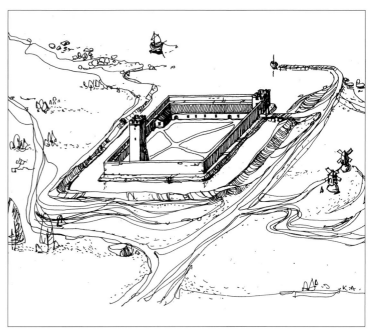

Swordbrothers captured Oesel island in 1227. Under the terms agreed with
Bishop Albert in 1204, the territory was reluctantly handed over to the Bishop of
Oesel-Wiek, and over the centuries that followed there were several attempts by
the Teutonic Order to regain the territory that they had originally captured.

Excavations suggest that the original stone structure consisted of a
rectangular wall enclosing a courtyard with a prominent corner tower. This
tower, which still stands, may be dated to 1262/63, the years following the
overthrow of the Oeselian rebellion. Within a comparatively short space of
time the Livonian Order had expressed its authority in stone. The tower is 87ft
tall and of 22ft square cross section. It was originally enclosed within a low
rectangular defensive wall between 6 and 7ft thick while a 60ft-wide moat was
fed from the sea. At the opposite corner from the tower was a gatehouse, the
only other large building in the complex. The southern wall of Arensburg
formed the northern wall of the harbour.

By the mid-14th century this single tower had become the corner tower of
a rectangular convent building erected in typical Teutonic Order style. The
Arensburg convent was almost square and measured 130ft along one side. The
castle was entered via steps at the gate entrance of the north-east wing. The
inner courtyard consisted of a two-storey cloister. From the cloister one entered
the living quarters (built originally for the Bishop of Oesel-Wiek) in the
north-west wing. Next was the refectory and then the chapel in the south-west
wing. Beyond this lay the well-equipped kitchen and dining area. From there
one went into the dormitory in the south-east wing. There was a further
dormitory in the north-east wing.

The inner convent courtyard took 40 years to build between 1338 and 1380,
so we may presume that the construction was interrupted by the unrest in
Estonia that followed the so-called St George's Night rebellion of 1343. In the
course of the alterations the outer walls that had protected the original tower
were retained, but the gatehouse lost its former functions and became a corner
tower. An additional outer wall was added sometime during the 15th century
to provide two wet moats. The wall included several round towers, open on the
inner sides, and a prominent round fully enclosed artillery tower that has been
dated to 1470. The final addition to the ensemble we see today were the angle
bastions that were added during the 17th century.

Bauske (Bauska)

Bauske (Bauska) provides the best example of the last phase of development in Livonian castle architecture. It was built during the period of tenure of Heidenreich Fink von Overberg, Master of the Livonian Order between 1439 and 1450. The first written records of its construction can be found in a letter from the Livonian Master to Reval in 1443. The Livonian Order built Bauske to consolidate its power in Semgallia and to control the border with Lithuania, which lies only a short distance away. Bauske's liveliest time, however, came during the century after the Livonian Order had disappeared. It was besieged in 1625 during the Polish–Swedish war, and again in 1685. In 1701, at the beginning of the Great Northern War, the Swedish King Charles XII used Bauske as a storage base and frontier guard post. It surrendered to the Russians in 1705, and in 1706 Peter the Great ordered it to be slighted.

Bauske was originally built in the shape of an irregular quadrangular fortress on a promontory where two rivers met. It had five towers connected by thick fortification walls that had garrison buildings attached to them on the inside. The entrance to the castle was at its eastern end, guarded by two four-storey towers. The towers were connected to each other above the gate, thus making them into a very solid gatehouse. A quadrangular extension joined the large semicircular tower from the other side. There was a prison in the cellars. During the 1670s part of the old castle was demolished to build a new palace for the Duke of Kurland. The ancient fortification walls that remained were incorporated into the design. The system of outer ramparts was extended and perfected at the end of the 18th century.

A model of Bauske (Bauska) castle as it was in the 17th century. The lower half of the castle in this view is the medieval castle of the Livonian Order. The upper half is the extension added for the Duke of Kurland. We also see the angle bastions of the outer defences.

Wenden (Cesis)

Wenden (Cesis) provides detailed evidence for successive stages in development of military fortifications in Livonia over the centuries. When the Swordbrothers first arrived in about 1207, as part of their pacification of the Aa (Gauja) valley they settled in a former pagan fortress across the river. Wenden grew stone by stone from 1208 onwards and soon became the headquarters of the Swordbrothers. The Teutonic Order took over Wenden, which acted as their headquarters from 1470 until the time of the Order's dissolution.

The initial core of Wenden castle is believed to be its north-west wing, of which only basement vaults hidden under the ground have survived. In this wing a hall and chapel were located. Towards the end of the 13th century the castle expanded, and the addition of other wings gave Wenden the characteristic convent appearance. There was originally only one tower. This was at the southern corner.

Wenden's fortifications grew considerably over the next two centuries. The Lademaher Tower in the outer wall was added during the second half of the fifteenth century. Two other towers appeared during the 16th century: the northern tower and the prominent south-eastern tower called 'Lange Hermann'. Outworks, including more towers, were also added at this time, making the approach to the castle deliberately intricate. The growing importance of firearms may be noted in the addition to the western tower of a cylindrical upper storey pierced by gunports. By the early 16th century Wenden castle acquired its finished appearance. It was surrounded on three sides by considerable fortifications, while on the west more modest walls rose above a deep ravine.

Riga

Building work began on the first castle of the Livonian Order on the banks of the Daugava River on 15 June 1330, a few months after the defeat of the citizens by the brethren. The capitulation treaty obliged the citizens of Riga to grant a site where a replacement might be built for the former Swordbrothers' castle of St George, destroyed during the fighting in 1297. The site they chose was currently occupied by the Hospital of the Holy Spirit, together with the city stables, a limekiln and a horse-operated mill. All were torn down to make room for Riga castle. Records of Teutonic Knights being stationed in Riga castle in 1343 confirm the date of completion. From this time until 1470 Riga castle was the main residence both of the Livonian Master and the Commander of the Order's army, after which they moved to Wenden. The archives and treasure of the Order were also kept there.

It is no longer possible to reconstruct the appearance of the 14th-century castle with any accuracy. It is not even known for certain whether or not the castle stood inside or outside the city walls. One square tower, now part of the Presidential Palace, still survives, and stretches of wall have been excavated.

A second Riga castle, completed for the Order in 1515 by the citizens as a result of another defeat at the Order's hands, provided the basis of what we see today. The terms of the treaty stated that the castle should be built within walls and should have towers, cellars, a chapel, living rooms and dining rooms for the master. In the courtyard was a well and bathhouse. It also had a Great Hall, a room that was to witness the formal dissolution of the Livonian Order in 1562.

The new Riga castle, completed only in 1515, as shown in a print of 1550. Riga was a massive convent-style building of almost square cross section. It has two round corner towers with conical roofs at opposite corners and one square corner tower, the survivor from the first castle. Different reconstructions place either a small square tower or a round tower at the remaining corner. The two confirmed round towers survive to this day. Unlike the prevailing Prussian model, the sewage tower projected from the centre of the wall into the Daugava rather than from a corner, terminating at a long wooden harbour wall.

The new Riga castle represented the final flowering of Livonian fortification techniques in the years when the Teutonic Order still existed. Centuries of war have wrought many changes, but it is far easier to reconstruct the likely appearance of the new Riga castle than the old one. A series of contemporary prints of Riga, where the castle appears as a detail to one side, enable us to trace these developments. In the late 19th century the architect Wilhelm Neumann tried to reconstruct a plan of the Order's castle using these drawings. Even though his attribution of room use has since proved to be somewhat inaccurate, his overall reconstruction has largely been accepted, although there is still some controversy over the number of towers that were of a round appearance. In Neumann's reconstruction Riga is presented as a massive convent-style building of almost square cross section. It has two round corner towers with conical roofs at opposite corners and one square corner tower, the survivor from the first castle. Different reconstructions place either a small square tower or a round tower at the remaining corner. The two confirmed round towers survive to this day. Both are now covered in painted rendering, but a small area of the rendering has been removed from the eastern tower to show the original stone masonry underneath. Unlike the prevailing Prussian model, the sewage tower projected from the centre of the wall into the Daugava rather than from a corner. Most illustrations show the sewage tower terminating at a long wooden harbour wall. There is a low outer wall within a narrow moat taken from the river. As befits such an important castle, the external finish is impeccable, with strong narrow windows. Semicircular artillery ports are visible in the round towers.

During the 17th century the Swedes built a modern fortification circuit round Riga that consisted of a series of angle bastions. In this print from 1638 we see how they completely enclosed Riga castle, which now looks dwarfed by the huge new walls.

In the century following the dissolution of the Order Riga castle received both attention and neglect from the occupying powers. These developments are outside the scope of this book, but one dramatic early change was the addition to the original Knights' castle of a complex pattern of angle bastions. This was the work of the Swedes in the late 17th century, and a print from 1638 shows the entire castle of the Livonian Order fitting neatly inside one of the huge angle bastions and looking very tiny indeed. Beyond it lies a warlike star-shaped citadel typical of 17th-century work. The final alteration was the enclosing of almost all the castle within a palace complex. This is how Riga castle appears today, with only the two massive round towers indicating the existence inside of the last castle of the Livonian Branch of the Teutonic Knights.

The ruins of the convent courtyard of Ronneburg (Rauna) in northern Latvia. Although much overgrown the ruins of Rauna still give a good idea of the outline of the castle.

The living site

The castle garrison

The castles of the Livonian Order were garrisoned by warrior monks who led lives that were both military and religious. The castles were often called convents, a term nowadays only applied to the religious houses of nuns.

Wenden (Cesis) was the headquarters of the Swordbrothers and for many years the headquarters of the Livonian Order also. As such it was the seat of the Livonian Master. Although subject to the Grand Master of the Teutonic Order, the Livonian Master was given complete authority in Livonia. Like the Grand Master in Prussia, he was elected by the brethren for a lifetime term of office. When not in Wenden he would be touring the Order's territories; visiting key sites like Fellin, Riga and the castles along the Daugava River to provide support for his hardworking Knights. The Semgallian and Kurland fortresses saw much less of him.

The Livonian Master exercised great authority, but his power was neither absolute nor unchallenged. It has been noted above how one master was murdered by a rival, and the year 1471 was to see the very rare spectacle of the deposition of a master. John Wolthuss of Herse had been elected master in January 1470, and his election was confirmed by the Grand Master of the Teutonic Order in March. But by October 1471 he was deposed and a list of his crimes was presented to the investigating officer sent from Prussia. The main accusations centred around his acquisition of personal wealth, partly to provide security in his old age, but also 'to embrace the pleasures of life, to accommodate his own unruly desires, and to stay with other disorderly people'. Apparently these intentions became known by gossip to the ordinary citizens of Livonia long before the members of the Livonian Chapter got to know about them. He had also set such a bad example to the brethren that discipline was rapidly deteriorating. To save the Order's good name the commanders of Livonia rescinded their vows to the master and appeared in arms at midnight in his bedchamber. They yanked him out of bed, put him in chains and took him without any proper judicial proceedings to a prison in the castle of Wenden where he later died. According to an unconfirmed report he was beaten to death in the dungeon a year after his arrest.

The responsibility for leading the Teutonic Knights into battle on behalf of Livonia fell upon the *Marschall* (Marshal) of the Order. The *Marschall* also had a seat on the Master's seven-man council, along with the *Tressler* (Treasurer) and other officials. There was also an annual chapter meeting at which each *Komtur* (castellan) and *Anwalt* (advocate) would be present. These two positions completed the Order's hierarchy.

The castellans or *Komturs* were individually responsible for a particular key castle, each of which governed a designated region. At the Order's height there were 22 of these *Komtureis*, 'commanderies', in Livonia. Because Livonia covered such a large area decision-making was often delegated down to *Komturei* level, so each region was like a tiny state on its own. The *Komtur* supervised the garrison, maintained the castle and organised patrols. He was also responsible for wide areas of administration from his castle, such as the collection of taxes and the supervision of justice. This gave him an overview of the strength and loyalty of the local people, who would seek refuge with him in times of war. He also had responsibility for daily garrison life, such as seeing that the castle had sufficient food, that stores of weapons and armour were adequate, and that the castle's defences were in good repair. Each castle was required to store enough supplies to withstand two years of siege.

The other important office associated with a castle was the advocate or *Anwalt*. The *Anwalts* had the civil responsibility of governing the native tribes within a *Komtur's* district. They also collected taxes. The advocates did not live in the *Komturei* but elsewhere, often a small castle with only a tiny garrison.

There was one major difference from the power structure in Prussia, where the Grand Master ruled supreme like any medieval prince. The Livonian Master was not only under the Grand Master, but technically subservient also to the Archbishop of Riga. This arose from the notorious agreement of 1204 concerning the division of conquered lands. This had been so successful from the Church's point of view that in the complex patchwork that was Livonia the archbishop owned more territory than the Order. However, the balance of power had changed dramatically since the pioneering days of Bishop Albert, and successive archbishops rarely had the military strength to back up any dispute with the Order. One factor was the recruitment of troops. The Teutonic Knights relied upon warrior monks who were comparatively cheap to run compared with the secular vassals on whom the archbishop was compelled to depend.

In addition to the ecclesiastical power of the Rigan archbishop, the bishops of Dorpat (Tartu), Oesel-Wiek (Saaaremaa and north-west Estonia) and Kurland maintained castles and fighting men of their own. But when it came to conflict with pagans or Russians they depended very heavily on the support of the Livonian Order and its regular influx of crusading reinforcements from Germany.

The first crusaders on the Livonian scene, the Swordbrothers, were men of mixed social origins. They, and their successors, tended to be recruited from the Lower German areas disregarded by Prussia such as Westphalia, the Ruhr and the Netherlands. Many were from the *ministeriale* class: knights who were often poor and landless, not pleasure-seeking nobles. For them warfare was a means of social advantage. In the eyes of one cynical chronicler they were just 'rich merchants, banned from Saxony for their crimes, who expected to live on their own without law or king'. On one memorable occasion the honourable birth of certain Livonian brethren was questioned and recorded in writing:

> The castellan of Reval – his mother ran away with a priest … and the castellan of Dünamünde … his father was a peasant and a boor … and the prior of Riga is a runaway monk who was once accepted into the Teutonic Order and later expelled.

There were probably never more than about 120 Swordbrothers in all, who were spread among six convents. Just like the Teutonic Knights, the most important members were knights who lived as monks or, more correctly, friars, because their duties took them out of their fortified monasteries. Each knight-brother took vows of poverty, chastity and obedience in the war against unbelievers and received a horse, armour, weapon and, clothing, and had a man-at-arms (sergeant) to assist him. These sergeants were warriors in their own right and often dressed and fought as knights. The infantry operated siege weapons, garrisoned the castles and fought in battle. In addition there were cooks, smiths, bakers and other servants. All these lower-class members wore simple dark clothing with the badge of the sword. The Teutonic Knights who took over their duties performed similar roles and shared the same simple but complete religious and military existence. This is described in detail in Fortress 11: *Crusader Castles of the Teutonic Knights (1) The red-brick castles of Prussia 1230–1466* (Osprey: Oxford, 2003).

The monastic life

The religious life of a castle centred round the chapel, where religious services were performed by the brothers in their roles as monks. Daily services between dawn and dusk marked the passage of time in a manner that any medieval monk would have recognised. One moving ceremony that would have taken place in a castle's chapel was the reception of a new brother into the Order's ranks. The candidate

The economic life of the Teutonic Knights in Latvia – The new castle of Riga 1515

The second Riga castle, which was finished in 1515, represents the final flowering of Livonian fortification techniques in the years when the Teutonic Order still existed. Riga is revealed as a massive convent-style building of almost square cross section. It has two round corner towers with conical roofs at opposite corners and one square corner tower, the survivor from the first castle. The sewage tower, very similar to the traditional design found in the castles of the Teutonic Knights of Prussia, projected from the centre of the wall into the Daugava River, terminating at a long wooden harbour wall. There is a low outer wall within a narrow moat taken from the river. As befits such an important castle, the external finish is impeccable, with strong narrow windows. Semicircular artillery ports are visible in the round towers.

would have received instruction from a brother in the duties that would be expected of him. He was expected to know the Creed and the Lord's Prayer, or would be taught them. On being introduced to the brothers he would kneel down in front of the entire chapter and beg to be admitted to the Order for the sake of his immortal soul. The Superior of the convent would then ask the postulant five questions that were derived directly from the Rule of the Templars. Do you belong to any other Order? Are you married? Have you any hidden physical infirmity? Are you in debt? Are you a serf? Having answered each question in the negative, the candidate would have to answer 'yes' to five more questions. Are you prepared to fight in the Holy Land? Are you prepared to fight elsewhere? Will you care for the sick? Will you practise any craft you know as ordered? Will you obey the Rule of the Order? He would then make his profession:

I, X, do profess and promise chastity, renunciation of property, and obedience, to God and to the Blessed Virgin Mary, and to you Brother Y, Master of the Teutonic Order, and to your successors, according to the Rules and Institutions of the Order, and I will be obedient to you, and to your successors, even unto death.

He would then be accepted for a period of novitiate, and the Order promised to him in its turn that it would supply him with bread, water and old clothes. The chronicler Peter of Dusburg claims that early brothers of the Teutonic Order were so humble that they accepted clothes made out of flour sacks.

Just as in Prussia the eating of communal meals in the castle's refectory was a vital part of the monastic life. For three days of the week meat was included. For three more days only eggs or dairy products supplied the protein, and Friday

Treiden (Turaida) shown in its ruined state prior to the modern reconstruction.

was a weekly fast day. There were many other fast days. The only exceptions were for the sick or the weak, for whom the meal could be enhanced. Eggs, milk, porridge and water formed the brothers' staple diet, washed down by plentiful supplies of beer.

The hospitality shown by the Order to visiting crusaders is illustrated by a description of the arrival of a new Master along with a number of young knights in Riga in 1280:

> A messenger came running there to inform the brothers that the master had come. Their horses were in the pasture and they sent for them quickly ... Then he rode with many escorts to Saint George's. That monastery lies within the city and the brothers live there. The Master bade the brothers sit down and they were served wine and mead. Then they rode back to their quarters. A few days after the brothers had ridden to meet him they advised him to inspect the land, so he rode through Livonia. He found many good castles there, well defended by brothers.

The castle as economic centre

The world of the Teutonic Order embraced commerce along with prayer and warfare. The economic base was agriculture and trade, and the proceeds of agricultural activity made their way into the castle in the form of taxes. One of the advantages possessed by the Order were their cogges: round-bottomed sailing ships that carried bulk cargo so safely and cheaply that German merchants were able to undersell all competitors and make the Baltic Sea into practically a German lake. The Order's fleet of ships sailed between Prussia and Estonia, and up the Daugava from Riga. They also went out on to the Baltic as far as Gotland to sell grain, amber, linen and wood. When times were good the Livonian Order exported rye among other products.

The individual castles dominated the economic life of their territories, although local taxes were never quite sufficient to meet all the Order's needs. The shortfall was made up by gifts from Germany. Tribes that had been loyal for several generations were taxed at a rate of three bushels of grain per farmstead. Other tribes paid twice this rate. A list of taxes and services performed for the Bishop of Oesel-Wiek in 1284 has survived, and the demands placed by the Order on its own territories cannot have been very different. The rates were two and a half marks and a hen from each taxable unit of farmland. There was also payment in kind, consisting of one day of ploughin;, two days of haymaking; providing beer; labouring on fortifications and houses where these had been destroyed by the enemy; and also providing military service.

Early records of the economic holdings of a typical convent are sparse, but in 1341 the Commander of Goldingen (Kuldiga) took an inventory. This important castle controlled the whole of Kurland. Of domestic animals there were 18 plough horses, 39 oxen and five cows in the stables, with a similar number in use out in the fields. One half-brother kept 49 cattle and 100 sheep. Another kept three horses. There were also 70 head of cattle on the nearby estate of Alswangen, and an additional 308 cows dispersed among the natives. Of war horses, there were 30 in the castle stables at Goldingen, and a further 37, with 21 foals, at Alswangen. Food supplies were noted as follows:

Rye
Goldingen – 70 barrels; Alswangen – 39 barrels; Hasenpoth – 27 barrels; Neuhaven – 15 barrels; Lyndal – 43 barrels; with the Bishop of Kurland – 2 barrels.
Wheat
Goldingen – 35 barrels; Windau – 114 barrels; Oesel – 122 barrels; Pernau – 100 barrels; Gotland – 92 barrels.

Other commodities
One barrel of hops ageing, two barrels ready for brewing; one half-barrel of honey for mead; 43 marks' worth of amber; 300 marks cash in hand.

The stores noted in outlying warehouses were kept for sale, not for the use of the castle garrison, which does not leave a huge amount of animals and food for a castle that had responsibility for a vast area.

It is interesting to compare the above list to a similar inventory taken at Goldingen over a century later in 1451. It reads as follows:

The food supplies of the castle: 57 barrels of wheat, 12 barrels of meal, 32 barrels of barley, 4 barrels of malt, 12 barrels of hay, 100 sides of bacon, 250 hams, 6 sides of dried beef, 28 sides of salted beef, 24 barrels of salt.

This inventory conveys no impression of luxury, and although the amount of food stored looks impressive, the total of 101 barrels of grain is slightly less than the 105 barrels of 1341. This probably reflects Goldingen's declining importance. The 1451 inventory for Goldingen also contains a reference to the small quantity of armaments kept in the castle. It reads:

Also in the castle are armour for 12 men, one barrel of arrows, half a barrel of powder and half a barrel of sulphur.

That same year Goldingen listed its garrison by name:

This is the garrison: John of Stemmen, a Westphalian is the Commander; Deputy Dietrich Plowicke of Geldern; two priest-brothers, Lord Gerhard Stecke of Cleves, Bernhard Schilling of the Bishopric of Munster.
[Lay brothers are] Henry of Walgard from Mark, Werner of Sunderick from the Bishopric of Paderborn, Isebrand of Bomgarten from the Archbishopric of Koln, John of Doessel from Berg, Andrew Anreip from the Bishopric of Paderborn, Waller of Almen from the Bishopric of Utrecht, John of Erthe from Brabant, William of Calleten from Bremen.
The sergeant [literally 'grey mantle'] Lucas, the sergeant Claus the shoe maker, the sergeant John the master baker.

Among the aforementioned men no one had armour or a horse except the commander.

Goldingen (Kuldiga) the most important castle in Kurland (Kurzeme), as it appeared in 1680. This is a classic square convent building surrounded by very strong outer walls.

Operational history

Siege warfare and the timber castles

We are fortunate that accounts of the early wars carried out by the Swordbrothers contain vivid descriptions of contemporary operations conducted against the original wooden castles that the Order's stone castles then replaced. Of particular value is the *Chronicle of Henry of Livonia*, which describes the methods used by the Swordbrothers to take the fight to the pagan hillforts. The Swordbrothers tended first to ravage the area around, killing the inhabitants, they then used archery to clear the enemy from the outer ring of defences while the moat was filled in. An assault, often using fire, would follow.

A good example dates from 1211. At Fellin (Viljandi) in Estonia, the stronghold of the Saccalians, a fierce attack was launched but went very much against the crusaders. The Estonians killed and captured several of the attackers and seized their armour and helmets. These they subsequently wore up on the ramparts for the besiegers to see. One advantage the crusaders seem to have had was in their archery, and they managed to drive the garrison back sufficiently to allow a respite to build a movable siege tower:

> The Livonians and Letts carried wood and filled the moat up from bottom to top, and pushed the tower over it. The Letts and the *ballistarii* went up on the tower, killed many men on the battlements with arrows and spears, wounded many, and for five days a great battle raged. The Estonians strove to burn down the first pile of wood by casting a great deal of fire from the fort on to the carts. The Livonians and Letts threw ice and snow and put it out. Arnold, a brother of the militia [i.e. a Swordbrother] laboured there day and night. At last he was hit by a stone and crossed over into the brotherhood of the martyrs. He was an extremely religious man and was always praying. He found, as we hope, that for which he prayed.

The *ballistarii* are likely to have been the twin-armed torsion catapults known to the Romans as *ballistae*. The crusader army then 'built a machine' and flung

An old postcard showing the ruins of Kokenhusen (Koknese) prior to the hydroelectric scheme. The castle ruins tower above the river valley.

stones into the fort. This machine was almost certainly a traction trebuchet, where a team of men pulling on ropes provided the motive power. The more familiar counterweight trebuchet was first used many decades later. Henry of Livonia tells us that these weapons were unfamiliar to the Estonians, so 'they had not strengthened their houses against the force of these missiles'. But even catapults were not enough to capture the fort:

> The Germans came down, brought flames to the fort and set it on fire. The Estonians pulled apart the flaming planks and the burning timbers of the wall and dragged them away. On the next day, when the burning was over, they replaced everything, and the survivors nerved themselves again for the defence. There were, however, many corpses of the slain in the fort, there was a shortage of water, and nearly everyone was wounded.

The ruins of Kokenhusen (Koknese) today. The rise in the water level of the Daugava has not dealt kindly with Koknese. Comparison with the earlier photograph shows the dramatic change over the years.

At Doblen (Dobele) in 1212 one siege tower was blown over in the wind, and we also hear of the besieging Knights digging at the ramparts. At Odenpah (Otepaa) they threw the corpses of captives into the water in order to pollute it. In another incident the defenders made use of the fact that the ground was frozen and:

> destroyed their bridges. This worked to their advantage later when the assault began, because the embankment was icy and slippery, and no one could get a foothold there. The Christians were thus unable to reach the wall, even though they tried hard enough.

Similar techniques continued to be used wherever timber structures were still to be found, as at Terweden in 1281:

> They plundered and ravaged the surrounding areas ... The next day a siege tower was devised, erected and moved forward to the moat ... Many cartloads of wood were brought up to fill the moat, and then it was all ignited. The castle burned in many places, but the fires were bravely extinguished.

Siege warfare and the stone castles

In 1185 the first stone castle in Livonia received its baptism of fire. This was Uexkull, and Henry of Livonia's brief account confirms how its construction helped the defence:

> At that time the Semgalls, pagans of the neighbourhood, hearing of the building made of stones, and not knowing that the stones were held together with cement, came with large ship's ropes, foolishly believing they could pull the fort into the Dvina. But they were wounded by the *ballistarii* instead and went away having suffered losses.

The *ballistarii* proved their worth again in the spring of 1206 when the castle of Holm (Salaspils) became a Russian target. It was the first western-style castle that the Russians had experienced, and Henry of Livonia writes that the

Russians were ignorant of the art of the *ballista*, being familiar, rather, with the hand-held bow:

> Yet they wounded many on the fortifications during the many days they fought and, bringing up a huge pile of wood, they tried to burn down the fort. Their labour was in vain, however, for many of them fell wounded by the *ballistarii* as they gathered wood.

Henry adds one other fascinating detail about the Russians' siege warfare:

> The Russians also made a little machine like that of the Germans, but not knowing the art of throwing rocks, they hurled them backwards and wounded many of their own men.

The description suggests that these machines were traction trebuchets. A further type of defensive weapon is noted when we read that the Russian advance against Riga was halted when they came upon the ground strewn with caltrops. Caltrops were simple iron spikes arranged in the shape of a tetrahedron so that one spike was always pointing upwards.

A typical spate of raiding and castle warfare accompanied the Oeselian Rebellion, the revolt that broke out following the news of the defeat of the Livonian Order at the battle of Durben in 1260. The commander of Segewold led an army to the north in the winter of 1260/61 and crossed 12 miles of frozen sea:

> Soon there were many great fires whose smoke seethed like storm clouds over all of Oesel. Many bold bands ravaged back and forth across the island and the natives were bereft of all joy.

The weakness of the old timber forts was soon demonstrated when some Oeselians retreated to a timber fort about five miles north of Arensburg. Crossbowmen were brought up 'and grimly advanced on the fort', which was soon taken.

Another incident involving the island of Oesel in February 1270 was to provide a dramatic example of what the word 'frontier' could mean in the context of the Baltic area. A powerful army under the new Grand Duke Traidenis of Lithuania raided Latvia and reached the coast of the Bay of Riga. They then decided to continue raiding as far as Oesel by marching across the frozen sea. The Livonian Master hurried to intercept them. His plans were to give battle on the ice. The survivors would be dispersed, and would probably perish on the way home across Livonia from cold or massacre. But the Lithuanians proved a match for the Teutonic Knights. They dismounted from their sleds and arrange them as a barricade for the moment when the heavy cavalry of the Knights charged at them. This was indeed a 'battle on the ice' reminiscent of the famous Lake Peipus in 1242! The frozen surface of the sea sustained a fierce conflict, but at the end of the brief hours of daylight the Lithuanians were victorious. Master Otto and many of his knights lay dead.

No castle was involved in that epic struggle, and in general the stone castles out on the borders proved to be so strong that they were to have very little operational history as such. The pagan tribesmen tried to avoid them wherever possible, and most accounts of fighting around stone castles concerns the Teutonic Knights taking on rivals with whom they were more evenly matched. The outstanding examples of such operations occurred in Riga during the disturbances of 1297 and 1330.

The 1297 incident was sparked when the Teutonic Knights destroyed the citizens' bridge. In the face of fierce opposition the Order strengthened the garrison of St George's with 500 men and began to construct a wall that would

Riga castle today. Riga castle was among the most important buildings in Livonia. It now houses the Latvian presidential palace and a number of museums. This view shows one of the original corner towers, and is taken from the modern bridge over the Daugava.

connect the castle with the two towers in the city wall that they controlled. The enraged citizens organised a demonstration outside the walls of St George's to protest, and stones were thrown against the castle, probably by hand. The Order responded by loosing volleys of crossbow bolts into the crowd with a contemptuous disregard for human life. Fire arrows followed the bolts and succeeded in burning down part of the city.

> The brothers attacked the city of Riga in a cruel and harsh manner from all sides with machines, arrows, lances, stones and other war engines, destroying all the buildings totally, and burning with fire the fruit trees, gardens and other planted areas, the meadows and fields.

When he heard the news the Livonian Master in Wenden was furious at the overreaction shown by his men, and the incident provoked fateful consequences. Having nothing further to lose the citizen's army returned the following day with siege equipment of their own, and within a few hours this unprofessional army had captured the castle of St George from the Livonian Order. They then began to demolish it. Certain reports, written long after the event, suggested that 60 knights were taken prisoner and beheaded, but the contemporary evidence points rather to a peaceful if ignominious surrender by the army that had cowed the mighty Semgallians.

Apart from such reverses, the crusader castles of Livonia provided secure bases from which the brethren could conduct siege operations of their own against enemies. These could be of quite long duration, and the peculiar problems associated with the lack of daylight in midwinter are acknowledged in a special privilege the Livonian Master obtained from the Pope in 1344. Having in mind the 'hard labours and infinite dangers' of the 'athletes of Christ and intrepid warriors against the pagans and infidels in Livonia' it was decided:

> that they be allowed to carry along portable altars for their priests or others, and in proper and decent places before a day is gone or while there is still light, to celebrate Mass.

Thus spiritually armed, the Teutonic Knights of Livonia would take the fight to the enemies of Christ. In the year 1390 this included joining their Prussian comrades for a siege of the Lithuanian capital Vilnius, an action that is also remembered for the participation of Henry, Earl of Derby, the future

53

The southern tower of Riga. The second castle, completed for the Order in 1515, provided the basis of what we see today. This is the old eastern tower.

King Henry IV of England. The Livonian brethren arrived on the eighth day of the siege. They were directed to the river bank where they built two bridges to support the attack. They then set out to ravage the countryside. But the siege did not go in the crusaders' favour. The city was strong, and the main defences of Vilnius consisted of two sections referred to by the Order's chronicler Posilge as the 'outer castle' and the 'walled castle'. The former was not walled and constructed only of wood. As it sheltered many inhabitants we may presume that this was the outer city wall of Vilnius. It was this area that first took the brunt of the crusaders' assault using the Livonian Order's bridges. After a few days of fierce fighting it was won, and both the English and German chroniclers praise the contribution made in the attack by Henry Earl of Derby and his English longbowmen. It was an Englishman who first planted his flag on the walls of Vilnius. Fire and terrible slaughter followed the victory.

The next objective was Vilnius castle itself. It would appear that what we now call the Lower Castle had been largely untouched up to this point and the crusaders now attempted to undermine it. The Upper Castle, being built on top of a rocky hill, would not have been an appropriate target for such endeavours. The precise machine used was a sow, a covered wagon on wheels that allowed miners to tunnel directly under the walls while the sow's roof protected them from missiles dropped from above. While the miners dug the English archers and some artillery kept up a fire against the defenders. But it was all to no avail. The garrison held out for two days short of five weeks and the crusaders withdrew.

It had been a long siege for a small expeditionary force and though the besiegers do not appear to have been discouraged by the lack of food supplies, their discomfort was still great. 'They stood five weeks in continual agony day and night,' says the chronicler Wigand of Marburg. Much of this was due to disease spreading through their ranks, but the end of the brief Baltic summer was fast approaching. Finally 'with all their powder shot away', as the chronicler puts it so succinctly, the crusader army abandoned the siege of Vilnius. The Grand Master sent the Livonians home first and then followed himself.

Siege operations in the Early Modern period

Whatever else was to blame for the collapse of the Livonian Branch of the Teutonic Knights following the battle of Ermes in 1560, it was not ignorance of modern defensive technology. By 1500 the Livonian Order controlled 60 castles in Latvia and Estonia, and many had been thoroughly modernised. After 1450 several castles sported massive round towers pierced by musket loops. Wenden and Riga were considerably altered by 1560. The city of Reval (Tallinn) acquired several artillery towers, including 'Kiek in de Kok' a six-storey tower that still stands today. The border fortress of Narva had angle bastions by 1560. When Dorpat (Tartu) fell in 1558 the Muscovites found 552 guns in the city armoury. Yet even these modern features were unable to withstand the Muscovite artillery.

The castle under siege – the developed convent style and harbour defences – Arensburg (Kuressaare) 1434

This plate shows the castle of Arensburg (Kuressaare) on Oesel (Saaremaa) Island in Estonia. It is under attack across the frozen sea from the Teutonic Knights of the Livonian Order in one of the many operations when it changed hands between the Order and the local Bishop of Oesel-Wiek. The southern wall formed the northern wall of the harbour. The original tower is the most important part of Arensburg. By the mid-14th century it had become the corner tower of a rectangular convent building. The Arensburg convent was almost square, measuring 130ft along one side. The outer walls that had protected the original tower were retained, but the gatehouse lost its former functions and became a corner tower. This is a difficult siege to maintain across such a tricky surface, and one assault party is struggling over the slippery ice.

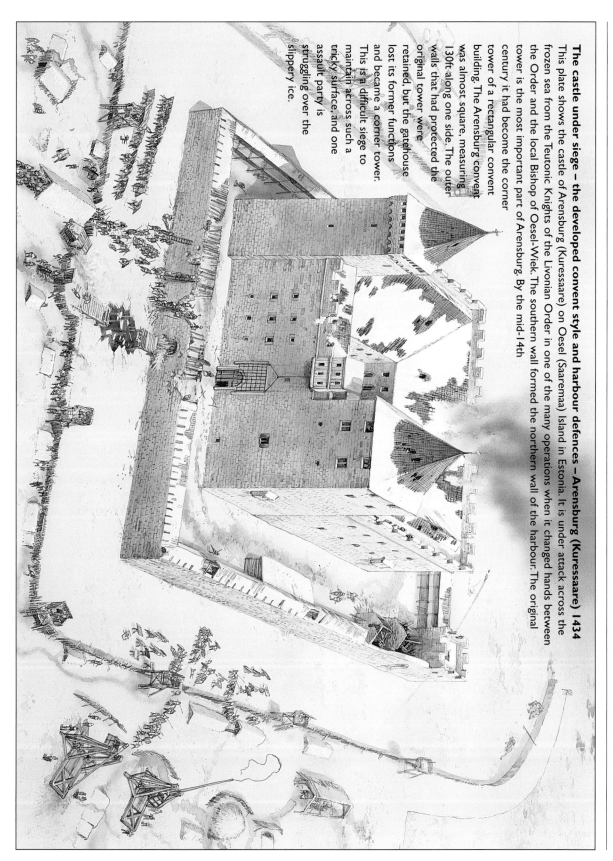

55

During the last century of the Order's existence Riga castle saw a great deal of action in particular, and accounts of the operations shed much light on siege warfare of the period. In May 1481 the Livonian Master fortified Riga castle against a further manifestation of unrest. Fearing the worst, he sent orders to Fellin, Wenden, Treiden and Segewold for them to lend their biggest guns to Riga. The citizens responded by nailing shut the city gates nearest to the castle. Both sides built new walls and dug ditches, and when hostilities began there was an artillery bombardment from each direction. The citizens were well supplied, possessed a giant mortar cast with the motto, 'I am called the Raven and upon whatever I lay an egg that breaks in two'. The Order's main cannon had a flat trajectory that prevented it from firing over the walls into the city itself, so they tricked the Rigan leader into entering no-man's land and blasted him to eternity with a volley of shot. The Rigans also raided the Order's possessions outside Riga, including the castles of Kokenhusen and Lennewarden.

An old photograph of the ruins of Ascheraden castle, which have long since been consumed by the rising waters of the Daugava River.

In March 1484, with the spring thaw approaching, the Rigans gave battle against the Order's Army while the weather conditions still favoured movement. They gained a victory, but old Riga castle still would not surrender to them, even though it had been reduced to a pile of rubble held together in some places only by chains. When it finally fell in 1484 only its outline remained. Once again the ensuing peace treaty required the citizens to rebuild it, but continuing political unrest meant that it took until 1515 for the new castle to be finished.

A fine model of Wenden (Cesis) castle as it would have appeared before the siege inflicted upon it by Ivan the Terrible in 1577. We are looking from the east. In the foreground is the Lange Hermann Tower, to the right of which is the convent block. A covered gateway and drawbridge give access over a wet moat. To the rear left is the West Tower, of which only the lower part remains today.

Aftermath

The secularisation of the Livonian Order did not mean the end of warlike activity in Livonia. The old crusader fortresses now became prizes in several centuries of conflict involving Poland, Sweden and Muscovy, who fought each other for what the the Order had left behind. In 1572 the Muscovites attacked northern Estonia and captured Weissenstein (Paide); they then had to defend Wesenberg (Rakvere) against the Swedes. In 1575 the Muscovites appeared beneath the walls of Reval but made no attempt to capture it. Instead another Muscovite army captured Pernau (Parnu) from the Poles in July. Between January and July of 1577 the Muscovites conducted an unsuccessful siege of Reval as a prelude to a summer onslaught led by Ivan the Terrible in person.

Ivan the Terrible's summer campaign took him into the former lands of the Teutonic Knights. His first incursion captured Dünaburg (Daugavpils) and Kokenhusen (Koknese), and then in late August he arrived at mighty Wenden. The town soon fell, but the castle held out until a traitor informed the Russians of the presence of underground passages beneath the castle. During the fierce resistance a cannonball nearly scored a direct hit on Ivan the Terrible. This enraged him, and he vowed an awful revenge for the moment when the castle finally fell. The garrison did not trouble to wait to see if he was serious, but took four tons of gunpowder and blew themselves to smithereens.

The loss of what had once been the Order's headquarters was an immense psychological blow to the defenders of the rest of Livonia. Only Reval, Riga and Oesel Island now held out, but this provided sufficient inspiration for their allies from Sweden and Poland/Lithuania to come to their aid. Wenden and Dünaburg were recaptured, but in September 1578 an 18,000-strong Muscovite army marched on Wenden once again, only to be decisively defeated. The attack involved yet another artillery barrage. Few castles can have taken such a battering in their history.

Many years of war were to follow as the lands of Latvia and Estonia were fought over. Centuries of conflict between Sweden, Russia and other neighbours took in the crusader castles of Livonia. But even as early as the 1580s the memory of the Teutonic Knights was rapidly fading, and few would even have heard of the Swordbrothers. Only their magnificent castles remained. They were damaged, rebuilt, transformed into palaces or modern angle bastion fortresses, and somehow seemed to resist every attempt to make them redundant. They stand today and preserve in stone the memory of the crusaders who built them.

The courtyard of Jaunpils, a castle that was not associated with the Teutonic Order. The illustration is included because this late medieval foundation, which soon became converted for purely domestic use, preserves a perfect medieval courtyard that would have been typical of the Order castles. Note the cloisters and the enclosed staircase.

The castle under siege – artillery against the developed form of stone castle – Ivan the Terrible at Wenden (Cesis) 1577

In this plate we see the siege of Wenden (Cesis) by the artillery of Ivan the Terrible in 1577. We are looking from the south side. To the right is the Lange Hermann tower, while in the centre is the fortified gatehouse that has since disappeared. Ivan the Terrible's gunners are operating from behind huge gabions of interwoven wood stuffed with soil. This reconstruction is based on the model in Riga castle that appears on page 56.

The Livonian crusader castles today

Following the collapse of the Soviet Union, Latvia and Estonia have become the proud independent countries they once were. Travel to both countries is easy, comfortable and readily available. City breaks may be taken in Riga and Tallinn, and longer trips are also most rewarding. Car hire is straightforward

Modern Latvia and Estonia shown in relation to neighbouring countries, with major modern roads and principle castles formerly owned by the Teutonic Knights. Note how the border between Latvia and Lithuania has remained virtually unchanged. (© Copyright Osprey Publishing Ltd)

N

BALTIC SEA

Tallinn (Reval)

E20

Narva

Rakvere (Wesenburg)

Paide (Weissenstein)

RUSSIA

Haapaslu (Harpsal)

Lake Peipus

ESTONIA

Saaremaa (Oesel)

Pärnu (Pernail)

Viljandi (Fellin)

Lake Pskov

Kuressaare (Arensburg)

GULF OF RIGA

Battle of Ermes 1560

A1

Valmiera (Wolmar)

A2

Ventspils (Windau)

Cesis (Wenden)

Sigulda (Segewold)

LATVIA

Kandava (Kandau)

Riga

Ikskile (Uexkull)

Koknese (Kokenhusen)

Kuldiga (Goldingen)

A12

Jelgava (Mitail)

Dvina River

Bauska (Bauske)

A7

LITHUANIA

Battle of the Saule 1236

0   50 miles
0   50 km

BELARUS

and the roads and hotels are good. The following list contains the modern names of the most important crusader castle sites associated with the Teutonic Order in Latvia and Estonia. I give the modern name first.

Bauska (Bauske)
Bauska is one of the best preserved ruins in Latvia and is important as an example of a late stone castle of the Livonian Order. The new castle, the palace of the Dukes of Kurland, is the first section that meets the visitor's eye. Behind it lies the majestic ruins of the old castle.

Cesis (Wenden)
Wenden was the Marienburg of the Livonian Branch of the Teutonic Order, and its magnificent ruins still testify to its importance. In 1383 Wenden joined the Hanseatic League, and prospered until being besieged by Ivan the Terrible in 1577. There is an interesting museum in the new castle just next door.

Dobele (Doblen)
This is a well-preserved ruin with many interesting points of detail. There is a good view of the site from the nearby bridge.

Ikskile (Uexkull)
The rise in the level of the Daugava because of hydroelectric schemes has meant that this castle, the first stone building in Latvia, now lies on an inaccessible island in the middle of the river.

Jaunpils
This late castle is more of a manor house than a fortress. It has since been converted into a stately home and is now a hotel. This has, however, preserved its charming inner courtyard, a feature that must have appeared in many of the Order's convents.

Koknese (Kokenhusen)
The rise in the water level of the Daugava has not dealt kindly with Koknese. Unlike Ikskile, where the river has preserved the site, the river at Koknese now laps at its foundations and threatens to take the few remaining ruins with it.

Plan of Wenden (Cesis). Towards the end of the 13th century the castle expanded, and the addition of other wings gave Wenden the characteristic convent appearance. There was originally only one tower. This was at the southern corner. Wenden's fortifications grew considerably over the next two centuries. The Lademaher Tower was added during the second half of the 15th century. The northern tower and the prominent south-eastern tower called 'Lange Hermann' appeared during the 16th century. Outerworks, including more towers, were also added at this time, making the approach to the castle deliberately intricate. It was surrounded on three sides by considerable fortifications, while on the west the more modest walls rose above a deep ravine.

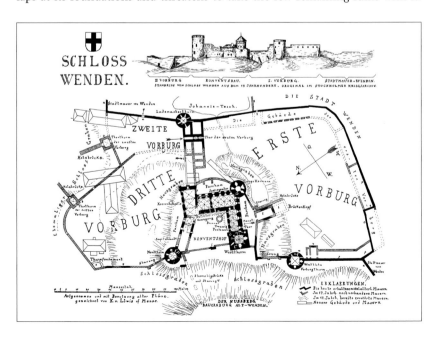

Comparisons with old photographs show the dramatic change over the years.

Krimulda (Kremon)
Only one wall stands on this overgrown site across the Gauja River from Sigulda. It was built between 1255 and 1273.

Krustpils (Kreuzburg)
The original Kreuzburg castle was built in 1237 and now presents the aspect of a later manor house.

Kuldiga (Goldingen)
The outer walls of this once important castle that controlled Kurland, built in 1242, have been preserved within the town of Kuldiga.

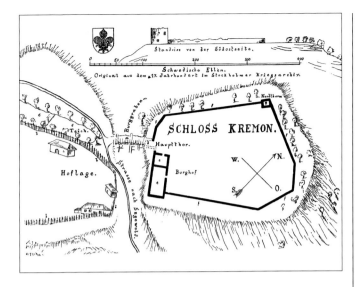

Kuressaare (Arensburg)
This huge castle complex on the island of Saaremaa (formerly Oesel) is one of the best preserved castle sites in Estonia.

Leilvarde (Lennewarden)
Located next to the Daugava in a wood, little remains of this once important castle originally built in stone in 1209. It is nonetheless worth visiting for the details it reveals of its construction.

Paide (Weissenstein)
The area in which Paide lies was ceded to the Livonian Order by the king of Denmark following the Treaty of Stensby in 1238. The building of Weissenstein castle followed in 1265. One huge tower, the Pikk Hermann, has been reconstructed after being blown up by the retreating Russians in 1941.

Rauna (Ronneberg)
The site, a few miles north of Cesis, is located on a wooded hill near the centre of the village. Although somewhat overgrown the outlines of the inner courtyard can be traced and provide an excellent case study.

Riga (St George)
Of the old castle of Riga founded by the Swordbrothers, only the former castle chapel of St George still stands. It has recently been very well restored and now houses the Museum of Decorative and Applied Arts.

Plan of Kremon (Krimulda), a modest stone structure built on a rocky plateau across the Aa (Gauja) River from Segewold. Its shape was an irregular hexagon of stone walls with a tower in the northern corner and other buildings in the southern corner. Otherwise there is nothing at Kremon of the developed convent style. Little is left of Kremon nowadays, but an examination of the ruins shows the utilisation of three types of building material in its construction. There are massive natural boulders for the foundations of the walls, which are finished using dressed stone and some red brick.

The castle of Kreuzburg (Krustpils) on the Daugava River. The original Kreuzburg castle was built in 1237 and now presents the aspect of a later manor house.

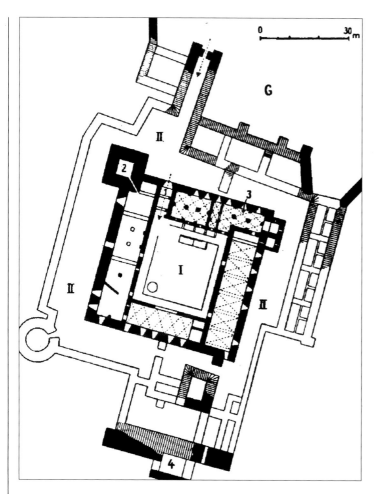

The convent building of Fellin (Viljandi). Ground-floor plan of the structure that fitted into the area described above.

Riga

Riga castle contains three superb museums including the Latvian History Museum, but most of the building is now the presidential palace and is closed to visitors. A good view may be obtained from the adjacent bridge.

Sigulda (Segewold)

The facade of Segewold is very striking, having been carefully restored, and shows excellent detail of the construction of the Livonian castles. It was built between 1207 and 1226.

Tervete (Terweden)

The earthwork of Terweden is superbly preserved in a lovely forest park.

Turaida (Treiden)

The hilltop site of Turaida has been extensively excavated, as a result of which part of the old Treiden castle has been rebuilt. Unlike almost all the other Livonian castles, Treiden was built largely out of bricks, which make it look more like its Prussian counterparts. The first non-timber castle was built here in 1214 by Bishop Albert. Nowadays much of the castle has been restored, but the use of machine-made bricks gives it a somewhat garish appearance.

Valmiera (Wolmar)

Little remains of old Wolmar castle, and its ruins are fenced off. It was quite a late foundation, dating from 1283.

Ventspils (Windau)

The castle site has recently been restored, but as a 16th-century palace in a rather alarming shade of canary yellow.

Viljandi (Fellin)

The stone ruins of Fellin are quite extensive, and are used for open-air concert performances.

A model of the original Turaida castle, a timber fort on a rocky plateau above the Aa (Gauja) River. This model is on display in Turaida Castle Museum.

Bibliography and further reading

Little has been published in English about the castles of Livonia. There are, however, several works that deal with the historical background. Outstanding among these are the books by William Urban that are listed below.

Aluve, Kalvi, *Kuressaare Linnus* (Tallinn, 1980)

Aluve, Kalvi, *Eesti Keskaegsed Linnused* (Tallinn, 1998)

Apals, J. et al., *Araisu Ezerpils* (Riga, 1998)

Benninghoven, F., *Der Orden der Schwertbruder* (Cologne-Graz, 1965)

Blomkvist, N. (ed.), *Culture Clash or Compromise? The Europeanisation of the Baltic Sea Area 1100–1400 AD (Papers of the XIth Visby Symposium 1996)* (Visby, 1998)

Brundage J. A. (trans.), *The Chronicle of Henry of Livonia* (Madison, 1961)

Caune, M., *Rigas Pils* (with summary in English) (Riga, 2001)

Kurlovics, G., *Latvijas Vesture* (Riga, 2000)

Lowis, K., *Fuhrer durch die Livlandische Schweiz* (Riga, 1912)

Ose, I., *Latvijas Viduslaiku Pilis (1) Petijumi par Rigas arhibiskapijas pilim* (Riga ,1999)

Smith, J. and Urban, W. (trans.), *The Livonian Rhymed Chronicle* (Chicago, 2001)

Turaida Museum, *Livs of the River Gauja* (Turaida, 1995)

Turnbull, Stephen, Campaign 122: *Tannenberg 1410* (Oxford, 2003)

Turnbull, Stephen, Fortress 11: *Crusader Castles of the Teutonic Knights (1) The red-brick castles of Prussia 1230–1466* (Oxford, 2003)

Urban, William, *The Livonian Crusade* (Washington DC, 1981)

Urban, William, *The Samogitian Crusade* (Washington DC, 1989)

Urban, William, *The Baltic Crusade* (Chicago, 1994)

Urban, William, *Tannenberg and After: Lithuania, Poland and the Teutonic Order in search of immortality* (Chicago, 1999)

The view of Doblen (Dobele) castle from the modern bridge, showing the good use made of the natural defensive position afforded by the riverside site.

Index